HPI

Essentials

A Just-the-Facts, Bottom-Line Primer on Human Performance Improvement

COLLECTION FEATURING

Dana Gaines Robinson

"Thiagi"

Mary Broad

Ethan Sanders

Joe Willmore

Carol Panza

Martha Boyd

George Piskurich

Holly Burkett

Tom LaBonte

Roger Main

Donald Ford

ASTD
Linking People,
Learning & Performance

George M. Piskurich, Editor

Ordering information: Books published by ASTD can be ordered by calling 800.628.2783 or 703.683.8100, or via the Website at store.astd.org.

Library of Congress Catalog Card Number: 2002105492

ISBN: 1-56286-315-0

Printed by Victor Graphics, Inc., Baltimore, MD

www.victorgraphics.com

Contents

Preface

This book was conceived and written to help those who are new to the discipline of human performance improvement (HPI) to build a basis for understanding the applications of the discipline. It is not a textbook as much as it is an HPI primer. In its chapters you will find very little theory but very much in the way of the practice and practical application of HPI as related by those who do it every day.

No doubt about it: Theory *is* important. The work of Gilbert, Harless, Rummler, and the many others who created the construct known as HPI is critical to a complete understanding of the field. The theoretical aspects of the discipline are covered in the founders' own writings and the multitude of books that have been engendered by their thoughts. This book goes one step further as it leads you through the essentials of *applying* those thoughts in your own organization.

Who Should Read This Book?

If you've picked up this book and are reading this preface, then you most likely have some interest in HPI. This book provides you with the practical introduction to the discipline that you may be looking for. The list of those who can benefit from it includes

- seasoned training professionals who wish to make the transition to HPI and need a book that gives them the basic outline of what they need to know
- new practitioners and students who want to learn more about HPI and need a short, easy-to-understand orientation to the field

- managers or administrators in HR, staff, or line positions who want to know what HPI is, how it works, and how it can help them in their business tasks.

How to Use the Book

This book meets the needs of those who are simply curious about HPI, know that they need to know more about it, feel threatened by it, or are just sitting on the fence while waiting for some guidance. Depending on which of these categories you fit into, you may choose to read singular chapters in priority order of your needs, or you may want to go cover to cover. Either way, this book will help you develop a basic understanding of what an HPI practitioner does—your first step in understanding the discipline.

Each chapter is written by a practitioner who is expert in his or her aspect of HPI. The chapters provide the basics of each topic and serve as a reference guide for further information, if and when you need it. They fill the gap between short journal articles that provide a simple description of various HPI topics and the larger handbooks and single-topic books that go into exhaustive detail.

How the Book Is Structured

As noted, this book provides the basics of the application of HPI as seen from the practitioner's point of view, or, more accurately, *points* of view. The book, like HPI itself, is not one voice but several, all with the same basic goal, but each speaking from his or her own perspective. Also like HPI, the path that each chapter follows to achieve its goal is somewhat different although the results are not.

The book is divided into 12 chapters, each one describing a different aspect of HPI. To help make the process a bit more understandable, the HPI model guides you as you work your way from analysis to evaluation. It is important to understand that this is not the only human performance technology model available, but it is a widely accepted one, and it lends much needed structure to your task of learning what HPI is all about.

Chapter 1. What Is HPI? What Makes a Performance Consultant? How Can You Tell if You Already Are One?

Ethan S. Sanders sets the stage by discussing a bit of the history of HPI and presenting the HPI model that guides your exploration of the field.

You'll see how HPI differs from other disciplines—particularly training—and be introduced to three of the basic principles of HPI.

Chapter 2. Business Analysis: The Driving Force Behind the HPI Process

Joe Willmore offers a "50,000-foot view" with a discussion of business analysis and how the organization's goals are critical to the HPI process. He explains why a business analysis is crucial to effective HPI, shows you how to conduct a business analysis as well as evaluate the results, and discusses how to avoid common mistakes many consultants make when conducting a business analysis.

Chapter 3. Performance Analysis: Linking It to the Job

Carol M. Panza's voice is that of the customer. In her chapter on performance analysis, she uses the customer to show us how to link business goals to organizational performance, while providing tools to help analyze both organizational and individual performance. She'll show you how to look at the macro level of the marketplace in relation to the organization and its key functional parts. Then, she helps you define performance context, discusses how to specify process as a sequence of accomplishments rather than behaviors, and illustrates how you can use the human performance system to ensure that all performance requirements link back to organizational goals.

Chapter 4. Gap Analysis: The Path From Today's Performance Reality to Tomorrow's Performance Dreams

Martha Boyd provides a unifying voice to all the various constructs of human performance through her discussion of the common, basic concept of gap analysis. She leads you through the role of gap analysis in HPI, describes how to conduct a gap analysis, and presents a number of critical issues that are associated with the process.

Chapter 5. Cause Analysis—Don't Assume Training Is the Answer, Don't Assume Anything!

In this chapter, the examination of HPI's systematic process continues by presenting methods for determining why the performance gaps exist. The discussion of cause analysis completes the analysis aspect of HPI by taking you through the purpose and methods of cause analysis and providing a simple job aid that you can use on your own, even if you are brand new to the discipline.

Chapter 6. Selecting an HPI Project: Finding an Early, Manageable Win

Tom LaBonte speaks with the voice of the client-consultant team as he reviews the critical HPI aspect of intervention selection. He leads you through ways of partnering with a client on a performance problem, selecting an intervention with a high probability of early success, and applying your skills and knowledge to a client intervention. His discussion sets the stage for the three very different voices of Thiagi, Roger Main, and Don Ford, who expand on Tom's overview with a look at the three major categories of HPI interventions.

Chapter 7. Motivational Interventions: Salary, Bonus, or That Corner Office

Sivasailam Thiagarajan, known to his legions of fans as Thiagi, takes a closer look at HPI interventions with a discussion of the category of motivational interventions. He helps you understand the critical features of motivational interventions, relates them to other types of HPI interventions, identifies different types of motivational interventions, and suggests a systematic approach to their development and implementation.

Chapter 8. Designing and Developing Structure/Process Interventions

Roger E. Main continues your introduction to interventions with a look at the structure and process interventions. He divides these into organizational and systems aspects, then drills even deeper into the process and job performer levels by discussing the basic components of a process and the various specific interventions that an HPI practitioner can apply.

Chapter 9. Knowledge Interventions: Training Is Not Always the Answer

Here, Donald J. Ford introduces you to the third and most recognized class of HPI interventions, knowledge interventions. He describes a seven-step process for designing knowledge interventions and an eight-step process for developing them. A knowledge intervention selection job aid is included to help you select the best learning, presentation, and distribution methods.

Chapter 10. The Research Is In: Stakeholder Involvement Is Critical

Mary Broad completes the HPI interventions aspect of the book by considering HPI implementation with the voice of one of the most important players in any HPI initiative, the stakeholder. She helps you recognize factors that support performance, identify key stakeholders, involve stakeholders in of the HPI process, identify specific strategies to support learning and performance on the job, and identify evaluation criteria by which you can measure the success of the change effort.

Chapter 11. Evaluation: Was Your HPI Project Worth the Effort?

Here, Holly Burkett discusses one of the stakeholder's most important concerns: evaluation. You will learn the benefits of implementing a results-based evaluation strategy, the steps required to build a credible, systemic evaluation plan, and how to apply a data collection template to an existing performance improvement project, all within the structure of a proven model for conducting evaluation at the level of return-on-investment.

Chapter 12. Performance Consultant—The Job

The voice of Dana Gaines Robinson caps your exploration of HPI by summarizing what it is that an HPI practitioner does. She helps you identify the four main accomplishments, or results, that are the focus of work for a performance consultant, understand the competencies used to select people into the position, and assess your own readiness to perform in the job of performance consultant.

In Sum

This book represents 12 different voices and perspectives, but they all have one goal in mind: to introduce you to the practical aspects of the process known as HPI. They all speak together about the practical applications of the basics of HPI and help you to take the first steps to understanding the discipline. It is my hope that you find these voices interesting and informative.

George M. Piskurich
July 2002

What Is HPI? What Makes a Performance Consultant? How Can You Tell if You Already Are One?

Ethan S. Sanders

If you are a hammer, everything tends to look like a nail.
— Author Unknown

Key Points

> Human performance improvement (HPI) is results-based and systematic.

> HPI does not follow a wants- or needs-based approach as training usually does.

> HPI uses cause analysis techniques.

> HPI focuses on accomplishments before behavior.

> HPI supports organizational goals by increasing the quality and quantity of individual outputs.

> HPI relies upon holistic systems thinking to examine organizations.

As business continues to evolve rapidly, the danger of certain occupations becoming obsolete increases. Although many professions are becoming more specialized (for example, medical specialties, computer application specialties, financial modeling specialties), there is also a greater need for generalists who can see the big picture, determine the correct skills to apply to a given problem, and coordinate the specialists' efforts.

In keeping with the vision of the performance consultant rising to a place of prominence in future organizations, remember that most decision makers today don't understand what human performance improvement (or human performance technology, or performance consulting, or performance engineering) is. Furthermore, it remains to be seen exactly who will be leading the charge toward a more scientific, data-driven approach to performance. Will it really be former trainers who just got sick of seeing their training efforts become mired in poor performance systems? Will it be some sort of HR manager who gets to know a specific part of the business and then performs triage when a line manager makes a request? Or, will some other discipline like finance or information technology grab the reins and declare itself the leader of the organization?

What it comes down to is this: Who cares? It doesn't matter whether an organization development (OD) or an HR practitioner follows the HPI process and principles—it's still HPI! It isn't the person's discipline or the words printed on a person's business card that makes him or her a performance consultant. In fact, many people who have "performance consultant" printed on their business cards really aren't practicing HPI. It doesn't take much probing to find out that they specialize in one sort of intervention (change management, process improvement, team building, or so forth) but are willing to consider *any* intervention request that comes their way. Yet, you can often find people who identify themselves as HR generalists or OD specialists who truly are performance consultants.

What Makes a Performance Consultant?

So then what distinguishes performance consultants from everyone else? The answer is very simple: their approach toward identifying and solving organizational problems. If they follow the HPI process and conduct themselves according to the underlying principles of HPI, they are performance consultants. The following sections describe the three primary principles of HPI and briefly explain the HPI model. It is essential to keep these principles in mind as you read through the rest of the book.

Principle 1: HPI Uses a Results-Based, Systematic Approach

Wow! What a mouthful! This first principle incorporates myriad elements surrounding the HPI model. Figure 1-1 outlines the three main approaches for trying to solve a performance problem, one of which is "results-based."

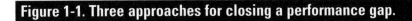

Figure 1-1. Three approaches for closing a performance gap.

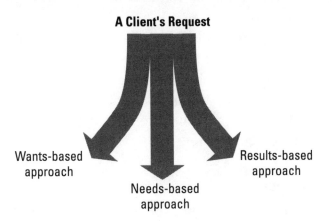

A Client's Request

Wants-based
approach

Needs-based
approach

Results-based
approach

Note that figure 1-1 does not specify *types* of activities or interventions, but rather the paths—or approaches—taken to *get to* an activity or intervention. Let's take a closer look at the differences between those paths.

The Wants-Based Approach

The term *wants-based approach* means that what the client wants, the client gets. You may ask questions to clarify what the client wants, but you never question whether or not the requested intervention will be of any long-term value. It's like playing a game of "Pin the Tail on the Donkey." It may solve the performance problem if you're lucky, but it may not.

A wants-based approach does not focus just on training. If your customer asks for new office furniture to raise morale, and you help him get it, this is still a wants-based approach. Remember that you cannot distinguish between HPI and any other HRD disciplines simply by considering the interventions that were used. For example, even if the interventions that an OD specialist offers are exactly the same as those a performance consultant offers, it's the manner in which the person arrived at those interventions that distinguishes the two.

Needs-Based Approach

The term *needs-based approach* refers to activities that are implemented in response to a specific performance gap. Unlike the wants-based approach, however, only those people with a documented performance gap are expected to participate in the intervention. There are numerous ways to identify performance gaps. Often a knowledge test is administered to employees in order to quantify who does and does not have the requisite skills. Other methods include observation of employees, recommendations from management, and analysis of performance data.

The problem with a needs-based approach is that it assumes that the customer has requested an activity or solution that will address the real problem—not just a symptom of the problem. Although the needs-based approach does not offer a blanket solution as does the wants-based approach, it still includes a prevailing belief—or an assumption—that the problem and solution have been correctly identified.

Results-Based Approach

Human performance improvement follows a *results-based approach* to improving performance, thus distinguishing it from most HRD activities. This approach must be driven by a business need and a performance need and must also be justified by the results of a cause analysis. The line of demarcation really is the cause analysis; you don't just assume that your client has correctly identified the problem. Of course, to conduct a proper cause analysis, a measurable performance gap must be identified, and a relationship between this performance gap and some organizational goal must be articulated. The results-based approach always works in the following sequence:

1. Identify an organizational problem.
2. Articulate a relationship between the problem and human performance.
3. Determine a quantifiable performance gap between the desired level of performance versus the actual level of performance.
4. Conduct an analysis of the root causes to reveal the reasons for the performance gap.
5. Implement a series of solutions to address the root causes.

HPI Is Systematic

Now that we have seen why HPI is results-based, let's address the idea that HPI uses a systematic approach. Human performance improvement is *systematic* because it consistently follows a process for articulating business goals, diagnosing performance problems, recommending targeted solutions and implementing those solutions, managing cultural issues, and evaluating the intervention's success. Figure 1-2 shows a model for the HPI process.

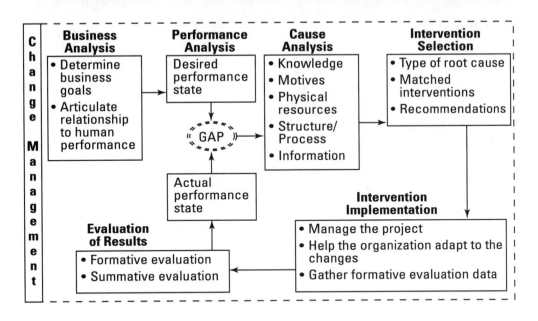

Figure 1-2. The HPI model.

It is this very model that represents HPI's systematic approach. Although it closely resembles other performance improvement models, this version contains some unique features. One of the dangers of using a model like this is that it appears to be sequential and linear when, in fact, only certain phases of the model actually occur in a specific order. The process is really only linear from business analysis through intervention implementation. Obviously, you can't recommend a solution if you haven't first identified the problem. Likewise, you can't uncover the root cause if you haven't first identified the performance gap. Moreover, you can't identify a performance gap without first knowing the business goal, the desired level of performance, and the actual level of performance. Change management and evaluation, however, must occur throughout the entire life cycle of the HPI project.

Principle 2: Begin by Focusing on Accomplishments Instead of Behavior

In light of HPI's results-based approach toward improving human performance, it is logical that performance consultants should calculate performance gaps in terms of accomplishments rather than in terms of behavior. Results and accomplishments are akin to each other in that the word *results* refers to the goals an organization strives for; and the term *accomplishments* refers to the specific outputs individuals are asked to achieve. Behavior refers only to the ways in which people perform tasks leading up to accomplishments.

When examining the performance levels of groups or individuals, accomplishments are much easier to detect and measure than behaviors because many behaviors are covert. Accomplishing goals—not just demonstrating particular behaviors—is what gets you to the desired business result. Furthermore, remember that the word *performance* is a noun that describes the execution and accomplishment of some activity; it is not an adjective that describes the action itself. The action itself is a collection of behaviors that may or may not add up to the desired accomplishment (depending on how things go).

It makes sense, therefore, to focus first on the desired end state (that is, the desired performance) before looking at the behaviors necessary to reach that performance: "Behavior is a necessary and integral part of performance, but we must not confuse the two. . . . To equate behavior and performance is like confusing a sale with a seller. . . . The sale is a unitary transaction, with properties all of its own, and we can know a great deal about it even though we know little—perhaps nothing at all—about the seller" (Gilbert, 1978). Certainly behavior does have an effect on performance, but it is premature to think about potential causes (of which behavior is only one) before determining the performance gap.

This distinction can be difficult for trainers to grasp. Although it is hoped that better-trained people will *accomplish* more, what trainers are really concentrating on is changing people's *behavior* through increased skill and knowledge. Kirkpatrick's (1998) four-level model of training evaluation is proof of this behavioral focus. As trainers, we are taught to evaluate interventions (which almost always come in the form of training classes) in the following way:

1. *Level 1: Assess the reaction.* Did the learners like the training and do they believe it was valuable? This level is usually measured through some sort of course evaluation form (for example, smile sheets).

2. *Level 2: Assess the learning.* How much skill and knowledge did learners gain as a result of taking the course? This level is usually measured through pre- and postintervention tests.

3. *Level 3: Assess changes in behavior.* Did the learners perform differently back on the job as a result of the training? This level is usually measured through observation or by noting supervisors' opinions.

4. *Level 4: Assess results.* What difference did the learner's behavioral changes make in the attainment of business goals? This level is usually measured through determining the final results that occurred because the participants attended the program (increased production, reduced turnover, higher profits, and so forth).

Note that not only does the third level of training evaluation focus on behavior, but also the fourth level assumes that all business results will be realized through behavioral changes on the part of the performers. This is misleading (because research tells us that about 80 percent of performance problems have more to do with the performance environment than with the individual performer), and it puts you in the impossible situation of trying to measure the effect that behavioral changes have on meaningful business indicators.

In ASTD's 2001 Benchmarking Service survey of training departments worldwide, less than 4 percent of training departments reported measuring the business results of their training programs. The reason for this is simple: They can't measure the business results because they never knew what the original goal was that generated the request for the training program! It's like trying to measure the effectiveness of a whatchamacallit! First you need to know what a whatchamacallit is supposed to do before you can measure its effect on business results.

Because most training requests originate through a wants-based or needs-based approach in which the client assumed that training was the correct solution, the goal was never articulated. In a results-based, accomplishment-oriented approach, the Kirkpatrick model is turned upside-down. With the HPI approach, you begin by assessing the desired business result and then figure out what people will have to accomplish to reach this goal.

Principle 3: Organizations Are Systems

One of the cornerstones of HPI is the idea of systems thinking. Over the past decade, the idea of looking holistically and strategically at organizational problems has been popularized by authors such as Geary Rummler, Chris Argyris, and Peter Senge. "The harder you push [on the system], the harder the system pushes back. . . . A name for this phenomenon is 'compensating feedback' when well-intentioned interventions call forth responses from the system that offset the benefits of the intervention" (Senge, 1990).

This is a dilemma we have faced for centuries. Although a practitioner can use his or her individual expertise to fix one component of an organization, it is far more difficult to predict what effect this change will have on other parts of the organization.

Geary Rummler and Alan Brache (1995) operationalize systems thinking by labeling and describing the three distinct parts of an organization's performance system: the organization level, the process level, and the job/performer level. The *organization level* of performance encompasses the relationship between the organization and its market, and it describes the major functions engaged in by the organization as depicted in the organizational chart of reporting relationships and departmental functions.

According to Rummler and Brache, the *process level* of performance considers the flow of work as it cuts across departments. When you look at the process level of performance, you consider such things as workflow, job design, required input and desired outputs, and outlying processes required to support the performance being analyzed. But since processes can only be efficiently executed by people, Rummler and Brache say that you must also consider the *job/performer level* of performance to gain a truly holistic understanding of an organization. The job/performer level focuses on such things as hiring and promotion, individual performance goals, and past levels of performance, just to name a few.

Combined, these three levels make up the operational fabric of an organization. Any successful intervention must target all three levels of performance to make a real and lasting difference in most organizations.

The HPI Journey

Boiling down 75 years' worth of theory into three principles is no easy task. Within each of the principles discussed above is a plethora of nuances that make HPI a scalable, replicable, and teachable approach for solving organizational problems. It is important, therefore, to view the practice of HPI principles and methods as a journey. As you read through the following chapters and as you begin to implement HPI in your organization, keep those three principles in mind. Your ability to successfully guide HPI projects will be greatly enhanced if you follow a structured approach and constantly check your progress against the organizational goals that you are trying to reach.

Your HPI Challenge

Becoming a performance consultant is much like becoming an artist in that you can refer to yourself by your new job title well before others recognize you in this capacity. Here are some important questions to ask before you commit to this type of profession.

✓ Do you really enjoy helping people solve their problems?

✓ Can you deal effectively with stressed-out people who are being asked to look introspectively at their performance?

✓ Do you like being a detective?

✓ Can you be tenacious enough to get people to consider nontraining interventions?

✓ Are you the type of person who needs closure with every project, or can you live with the ambivalence of trying to reach goals that often change and shift as you move through the process?

References

Gilbert, T. (1978). *Human Competence: Engineering Worthy Performance*. New York: McGraw-Hill.

Kirkpatrick, D.L. (1998). *Evaluating Training Programs: The Four Levels* (2d edition). San Francisco: Berrett-Koehler.

Rummler, G.A., and A.P. Brache. (1995). *Performance Improvement: How to Manage the White Space on the Organization Chart* (2d edition). San Francisco: Jossey-Bass.

Senge, P. (1990). *The Fifth Discipline: The Art and Practice of the Learning Organization.* New York: Currency Doubleday.

About the Author

Ethan S. Sanders is president and CEO of Sundial Learning Systems. Before founding this company, Sanders was the manager of instructional design for ASTD where he led the research and writing of two major competency studies and redesigned several of ASTD's courses.

He is the co-author of *ASTD Models for Learning Technologies, ASTD Models for Workplace Learning and Performance, Performance Intervention Maps: 36 Strategies for Solving Your Organization's Problems,* and the ASTD course "Human Performance Improvement in the Workplace." He holds a master's degree in applied behavior science from Johns Hopkins University.

Sanders can be reached at Sundial Learning Systems, 1805 Commonwealth Avenue, Alexandria, Virginia, 22301; telephone 703.739.4344; email: esanders@sundiallearning.com.

Business Analysis: The Driving Force Behind the HPI Process

Joe Willmore

Key Points

- Business analysis is the process of identifying and clarifying key organizational goals, targets, or needs.
- Business analysis tells you what matters most to the organization you're working with.
- A business analysis includes identifying important goals for the appropriate business unit, clarifying that these are appropriate goals, and determining how specific and measurable they are.
- A proper business analysis should produce goals that you believe (and your clients agree) represent critical targets for the organization or business unit.
- The three stages of the business analysis process are entry, data collection, and agreement.
- Develop in advance a series of questions to ask if you want to ensure a proper business analysis.

The business analysis is the start of the HPI process. The business analysis is also more than just the beginning of the sequence; it is the driver of the HPI process. Though often misunderstood, the business analysis sequence of the HPI process is actually easy to grasp, and once you have this element of the process down, everything else will come much easier. So let's take a look at what is meant by business analysis and why it matters so much to the HPI process.

What Is Business Analysis?

Business analysis is the process of identifying and clarifying primary organizational goals, targets, or needs. Almost all organizations (profit and nonprofit, large and small) have a wide range of goals. These goals can exist at a variety of levels within the organization and hold varying degrees of importance: organization-wide strategic initiatives, the quarterly sales targets for the eastern region, or the department finance team's deliverables for the month. These are all examples of business issues to which some or all members of the organization are committed.

Some points about terminology: As you read material about HPI, you'll come across terms that are useful to understand. Some HPI professionals distinguish between business goals and business needs. For this chapter, you don't need to be concerned with this distinction because the business analysis addresses both issues. However, to provide you with useful background information, typically the term *business goal* refers to the target, objective, or strategic priority within an organization or business unit. *Business need* often refers to the gap that exists between the present status of the business (current business results) and the business goal (the intended or desired results).

Why Worry About a Business Analysis?

Traditionally, many trainers, facilitators, OD professionals, and consultants have not focused on the business targets of the organization. If a client requested a service (such as management training, an off-site retreat, or a team-building intervention), most consultants simply honored the request, assuming that the client knew best. More recently, however, trainers and consultants emphasize the importance of conducting a needs assessment, both to ensure that the training fits the culture of the group and to verify that a performance problem exists as the client claims. Nevertheless, the needs assessment is inadequate to justify any action and does not provide the information necessary for a successful HPI initiative.

The business analysis reveals what's important to the organization—its priorities, targets, and concerns (or what it should be concerned about). Any human performance issues (what people do or don't know, what they can or can't do, how consistently and how much they produce) are important only to the extent they affect business goals. For example, a needs assessment may reveal that the organization's managers are poor writers. However, before you rush out and begin designing an effective writing course, you must verify that the managers' writing performance matters to the organization, that some essential initiative or goal is not being met because the managers cannot write clearly.

Business analysis is important to the HPI process for two reasons. First, the business goals are the drivers for the organization. A business analysis makes clear what matters to the organization and what does not. Unless you know that, you cannot judge if your efforts will make a meaningful contribution to the organization. Second, the business analysis determines what performance issues are paramount and how to allocate resources wisely. There are plenty of performance issues or gaps in any organization—even high-performing and successful ones. Rather than look for apparent knowledge or skill gaps, you must identify human performance issues that affect important business outcomes. If you don't, precious resources may be wasted on initiatives that make little or no difference to the organization.

Dissecting Business Analysis

The business analysis consists of three main tasks:

- identifying important goals for the appropriate business unit
- clarifying that these are indeed appropriate goals
- determining how specific and measurable the goals are.

Identifying business goals can be easy if the organization has a clear focus and obvious priorities. Clarifying the appropriateness of goals sometimes becomes an issue because leaders or organizations need to change their targets, or they may claim allegiance to goals that aren't realistic or appropriate. You may also find situations where senior management isn't able to agree on organizational goals (or may actively pursue contradictory policies). Determining the specificity and measurability of business goals may also involve refining objectives so that evaluation and measurement is possible (especially after you've taken action).

It is not enough for you, the performance consultant, to identify what you believe to be appropriate goals. You need buy-in and agreement from your clients. The business analysis process sometimes involves negotiation and exploration with clients. You may quickly discover that goals stated on paper or in an annual report don't really exist, or the leaders may have different perceptions about what the goals mean. Sometimes the targets are out-of-date or unrealistic, and sometimes leaders are blind to new opportunities. In such situations, you may also have to inform the organization of what its goals should be.

As you carry out the business analysis, you will inevitably gather industry- and business-related information on a series of issues such as:

- the external and internal factors that shape business goals
- the organizational rationale for those goals
- significant trends and forces within the industry
- relevant strategies to attain business goals.

The degree and level to which all of this information is gathered depends upon your judgment. As a performance consultant, you'll adjust your business analysis to fit the particular circumstances you face. Therefore, in some cases your business analysis will focus on companywide goals; in other cases you will focus on unit- or team-specific or, perhaps, short-term needs. Obviously, the more business acumen and knowledge of the organization's industry that you possess, the easier you'll find the business analysis process to be.

Assessing Your Business Analysis

How do you know if you've done an effective business analysis? First, your business analysis should have produced a goal or goals that you believe (and your clients agree) represent prime targets for the organization or business unit. That means that the goal or goals ideally should be

- measurable so that you can track progress and evaluate results
- time-bound to indicate when the goal should be reached
- output-focused (for example, to increase sales, decrease rework, shorten cycle times, or improve customer retention)
- important and relevant to your client so that the organization believes that progress in that area would constitute a success.

How NOT to Do a Business Analysis

Don't fall prey to common mistakes that can allow otherwise smart trainers and HRD professionals to convince themselves that they have conducted an effective business analysis when, in fact, they have not. Here are three bits of advice for your business analyses:

1. You can't assume that just because knowledge and skills are good for the organization that your actions to improve knowledge and skills will necessarily help the organization reach its business goals. If the new knowledge or enhanced skills aren't relevant to key organizational goals, then the business need still persists and you may have wasted resources on lower priorities.

2. Don't take it for granted that the client knows the organization best and that you can trust the client's conclusions about business needs or the priorities of those needs. Many OD professionals fall victim to clients who ask for particular interventions (such as team-building activities), assuming that the client wouldn't ask for a particular intervention unless it was important to the organization. If the client knew everything, then there would be little need for a business analysis or the subsequent performance analysis. Whatever you are initially told by the client needs to be checked by your own business analysis.

3. Don't try to rationalize a business need for a particular intervention. If you start with the action or intervention (whether it is training or any other activity) and look for ways that it would be beneficial, it is usually possible to come up with a rationalization to justify the action. If a client comes to you and requests time management training, you can usually find a way to show how that particular training links to and thereby supports almost any goal within the organization. Instead, you need to start with the business goals and then undertake a performance analysis. Once you've determined what performance is key to the business goal, you'll have a much clearer idea of the relevance and value of a specific intervention.

Second, your business analysis should also provide you with a better understanding and background of the organizational strategy and business environment issues to be able to identify the following:

- the organization's rationale behind the goal and why it is a priority
- other organizational goals, including ones that may be competing or contradictory goals within the organization
- other strategies that have been identified or tried previously to meet this goal.

How the Business Analysis Process Works

The actual process that you use to conduct a business analysis varies with the nature of the organization, its size, the range of goals, and the clarity of the goals. In general, though, the business analysis process consists of three stages: entry, data collection, and agreement.

Stage 1: Entry

In this stage, either you approach the client or the client contacts you and you meet to discuss perceived problems and ways you can help. During this discussion, clients often seek your commitment to provide specific actions or interventions with the result of short-circuiting the HPI process. Despite the client's interest in jumping immediately to solutions, you must find ways to bring the conversation back to the strategic priorities of the client.

Stage 2: Data Collection

After the initial entry into the organization, you'll begin to identify the relevant business goals through an information-gathering process. Depending upon the alignment of the organization and confusion around the goals, the process may be quick or it may be a little more demanding. Table 2-1 lists some of the questions that you need to address during this stage of business analysis.

Typically, a performance consultant uses a combination of executive interviews, document review (annual reports, strategic plans, individual/team and department plans), and survey/focus groups. Sometimes external or competitor analysis can identify relevant forces and issues outside the organization's walls. You may discover (if you're dealing with a business unit that is part of a much larger organization) that you need to go above your client's head to gain access to the people to whom the client reports.

This stage of the process is one that calls for you to use your judgment. If the client appears to have a strong, clear focus and if you can quickly verify

Table 2-1. The most important questions to ask for the business analysis.

1. How important is this goal to the business? How do you know the degree of importance?
2. Are there alternative goals that warrant more attention than the goal targeted by your client?
3. To what extent is the goal congruent with business strategy, values, and other goals? Are there competing goals? Are there goals that supersede this one?
4. Is the goal likely to remain stable?
5. What degree of buy-in on this goal is there by stakeholders?
6. To what extent are business goals supported by reliable and valid data?
7. How does the organization measure progress on the goal at present?
8. What forces (external and internal) are working for and against achievement of this goal?

that other sources are consistent with the client's perspective, your data collection stage will go quickly.

Stage 3: Agreement

The third stage involves returning to the client with your findings and seeking common ground and clarification. In some cases, this stage may be quick because you have verified what the client already knew. In other instances, you have to persuade the client that his or her goals are artificial or misguided and that the true direction of the organization is reflected in your report. Or, you may need to seek clarification about how to interpret particular data because managers or personnel may perceive the same goal to mean different things.

In any case, when you're finished with this stage, you should have a clear business goal and any background information on the business strategy and environment that is relevant to your ability to understand issues around the business goal. More important, you'll have laid the groundwork for evaluating the results of your work, and you and the client now share a common sense of priorities and direction.

Distinguishing Between a Business Need and a Performance Need

Subsequent chapters specifically cover performance and performance gaps. At this stage, suffice it to say that the business goal is the objective that the organization or business unit seeks to achieve. The human performance component involves the tasks and behavior that lead to that business goal. In other words, *the business need or goal is an end or desired achievement, whereas the human performance need or performance target enables the organization to meet that business goal.*

For example, the recruiting staff within the HR department seeks to improve its performance filling positions within the sales department. The performance goal could be stated this way: Fill all sales-related vacancies within two weeks of being listed. The business goal behind the need for HR to fill these vacancies quicker could be phrased thus: To increase sales by 8 percent in the next quarter and 23 percent for the fiscal year.

Cautionary Tales: Don't Let This Happen to You!

Let's look at some examples that illustrate both the importance of the business analysis as well as mistakes to avoid. Both cases briefly refer to other issues (such as the performance analysis, cause analysis, and evaluation) that will be covered in more detail in subsequent chapters.

Case 1: Wasted Resources

Anna is a performance consultant who works in a large, multinational organization. After the latest senior management retreat, she is informed that management believes there is a strong need for better communication skills within the organization. Doing a competency study and a needs assessment, Anna discovers that employees in the organization do tend to have poor communication skills and are aware that they could interact more clearly and effectively.

Benchmarking and Other Successes. Anna examines communication programs in many other organizations, identifying outstanding elements from these programs. She designs a series of communication skills seminars that have clear objectives, are very interactive, and have material that is specific to work. The pilot workshop receives high evaluations from participants who enjoy it very much. But, Anna isn't satisfied with that; she follows up by observing participants from the pilot workshop on the job and then meets with their supervisors. The feedback is unanimous: All participants have significantly improved their communication abilities and they are behaving differently on the job. This is gratifying news to Anna who has spent the past six months doing nothing but working on this communication skills training initiative. It has taken all of her time and budget for the past two quarters.

Success? It would seem that Anna's efforts have been a smashing success, yet she has actually failed despite providing a program the client requested, receiving good reviews, and demonstrating a significant improvement in participant skills. A corporate cost-cutting effort at the end of the year concluded that Anna and her office had contributed little value to the organization despite her efforts.

Where Did Anna Go Wrong? Anna failed to do any kind of a business analysis. Despite the request by the client (senior management) to provide communication skills training, she had no idea what the organizational goals were for the year or even the upcoming quarter. Therefore, she had no idea how communication skills related to any of those priorities. Just because senior management requests an action or intervention does not make it a business goal.

An improvement in communication skills, although laudable, may not have any effect on major organizational initiatives. Anna spent all of her time and resources on something that had little or no value to her organization. If she had taken the time to do a business analysis, she would have not only learned about important strategies and issues that could have facilitated the implementation of her program, she also would have been aware of what the priority targets were for the company. This knowledge would have allowed her to ask intelligent questions about whether communication skills were a relevant or effective way to achieve that business goal.

Case 2: False Reasoning

In analyzing his organization, Raul concludes that there is too much wasted time. Accordingly, he is proposing that all personnel acquire personal digital assistants (such as Palm Pilots), receive job aids to help them use these personal organizers, and attend mandatory time management training. But, Raul knows he is supposed to do a business analysis. He's aware that the top organizational goals for the year are to increase sales and shorten the delivery cycle once orders are placed.

Reasoning Sounds Good. Raul thinks to himself, "If the sales representatives waste less time, they'll be able to make more sales calls, thereby increasing sales. So, my initiative certainly supports our first corporate goal—to increase sales." When he reflects on the second goal (shorten delivery cycle), Raul concludes, "The Palm Pilots will minimize disorganization, and people can use the calendar feature to keep on the delivery schedule. The Palm Pilots will help with the second business goal as well!' Raul gets approval for his initiative.

Palm Pilots for All. Across the company, almost everyone loves getting a Palm Pilot, and the managers agree that their staff need time management training. Initial approval is high. At the end of the year, though, sales are down and the delivery cycle hasn't gotten any shorter. Raul is dumbfounded! Where did he go wrong?

Where Did Raul Go Wrong? Raul started his business analysis on the wrong end by beginning with the initiative or intervention (time management training and new job tools) and rationalizing his way to the business goals. He should have started by looking at the business goals: increasing sales and shortening the delivery cycle. If he had initially asked, "What has the greatest effect on our sales?" he would have found out his company's product is overpriced compared to the competition. Unfortunately for Raul, helping the sales representative become more efficient, allowing them to make more sales calls, didn't net significantly more sales.

Palm Pilots Are Mere Toys. An accurate business analysis might also have told him that when sales people (and other employees) were left alone with the Palm Pilots they played games on them, thus decreasing their efficiency and productivity. If he had started by looking at the delivery cycle and identifying the factors that affect the cycle most, Raul would have discovered that time management by employees was irrelevant. Instead, delays in delivery of parts from a subsidiary led to backlogs in the delivery cycle. Although all these issues relate to both the performance analysis and gap analysis chapters, they also demonstrate how easy it is to rationalize that an intervention will make a difference in a strategic goal—if you start by looking at the action rather than looking at the business goal.

Your HPI Challenge

The best way to improve your ability to identify business goals and apply them to the HPI process is to practice applying these concepts. So, before you actually have to identify a business goal for a work-related project, answer the following challenges.

✓ Identify at least one example of an intervention (training or non-training) in your organization that was apparently delivered without a business analysis and appears to have no relationship to any business goal (for example, offering a training class for a software package that isn't used by the company).

_____

_____

✓ Identify at least one example of an intervention (training or non-training) that was justified as relevant to a business goal by starting with the intervention and working up to the goal, rather than starting with the business goal. For instance, a stress management course, which was justified as a response to employee retention problems, can be rationalized as having a link to a business priority (retention). However, if you looked at the business goal (retention) and asked what performance gaps (and causes) contribute to the lack of retention, you would identify many factors. These factors might include better wages being offered by competitors, an adversarial organizational culture, and few opportunities for promotion. In such a case, managing stress better wouldn't appear to affect retention at all.

_____

_____

_____

_____

✓ Identify an organization with a substantial internal training program. Determine what the major business goals are for that organization.

Working backward from those goals, how closely aligned is the training with those business goals?

_____

_____

_____

_____

_____

_____

_____

_____

Additional Resources

Langdon, D. (2000). *Aligning Performance: Improving People, Systems, and Organizations.* San Francisco: Jossey-Bass/Pfeiffer.

Robinson, D.G., and J. Robinson (editors). (1998). *Moving From Training to Performance.* Alexandria, VA: ASTD.

Robinson, D.G., and J. Robinson. (1995). *Performance Consulting: Moving Beyond Training.* San Francisco: Berrett-Koehler.

Sparhawk, S. (1994). "Strategic Needs Analysis." *Info-line* Issue No. 9408.

About the Author

Joe Willmore is the 2001–2002 chair of the ASTD National Advisors Chapter and also serves on the ASTD board of directors. He is president of the Willmore Consulting Group, a performance consulting firm with headquarters sited in Annandale, Virginia. Previous clients include the World Bank, Smithsonian Institution, National Geographic Society, Lockheed-Martin, TRW, and U.S. Geologic Survey. He has also been a facilitator for the ASTD HPI certificate program.

Performance Analysis: Linking It to the Job

Carol M. Panza

Key Points

> ➤ The only practical source for developing measurement standards or criteria is the customer marketplace.
> ➤ Organizational performance can be improved by clarifying and managing the customer-supplier relationships that join the component parts (internal functions) of any company.
> ➤ Performance analysis must proceed along a macro-to-micro analysis path.
> ➤ An accomplishment focus for process specification is the only way that you can build an analysis framework for processes that can both accurately define those processes and also remain open to continuous improvement.
> ➤ People/performers must be specifically addressed in analysis because people are the organization.

Whether you're talking about the whole organization, a function, department, work process, or even a position, performance is measured by results—

what gets produced and is valued by internal or external customers. Performance analysis is critical to any organization's ability to improve its results and, ideally, achieve important goals and objectives. In fact, any organization that fails to commit itself in a meaningful way to continuous improvement will certainly not become or remain a leader. It is highly unlikely for such an organization to be competitive within its marketplace.

By the way, using the word *marketplace* does not assume that all organizations have a profit motive. It does mean, however, that all organizations have customers who are the reason for the organization's existence and the recipients of its products or services. Furthermore, customer focus is not limited to the organization level. All functions, work processes, and positions have customers as well and should be viewed as forming an internal customer-supplier network designed to support the organization's success with external customers. This viewpoint leads to a very fundamental concept: Just as performance analysis is critical to continuous improvement, customer focus is essential to useful performance analysis.

Three Important Concepts

The approach used in this chapter for performance analysis is characterized by three important concepts:

1. Start with the marketplace context and a relationship view of the organization rather than a focus on process specification.

2. Specify process as a sequence of accomplishments versus behaviors or just stuff.

3. Use the human performance system to ensure that all performance requirements and any changes are linked back to organizationally desirable goals and that the performers are properly supported.

The first concept means that you need to start at the macro level to view the organization and its major functional parts in the context of the marketplace in which it operates, that is, the organization's current and potential customers, suppliers, competitors, and regulatory authorities. Defining performance context is the essential first step, whether the organization has a profit goal or not. And, this definition must precede analysis and improvement actions focused on processes, even critical cross-functional processes, to avoid the risk of optimizing one part of the organization at the expense of others and, consequently, the whole organization.

The second concept stems from Gilbert's (1978) concept that accomplishments are the key to understanding performance requirements in a useful, manageable way and then specifying performer expectations. By applying this important concept to process analysis, you can see that process specification needs to be an articulation of the series of accomplishments or outputs required for producing a valued product or service. This philosophy stands in contrast to the more usual sequence of actions or behaviors—what people do rather than what they must get done or accomplish. An accomplishment focus can help you avoid a common pitfall: namely, focusing on and cementing into place the most current tools and techniques. No matter how up-to-date, tools and techniques change while the outcomes that result from these actions or behaviors remain the same almost indefinitely. When accomplishment-based process descriptions are developed for the key internal and external products and services produced by an organization, what you have is a practical framework for specification of useful performance-based position requirements. Stated another way, process descriptions form the essential link between organizationally desirable outcomes required at the macro level, and jobs/positions at the performer level.

The third concept means that people must be specifically addressed because they *are* the organization. The human performance system model (figure 3-6) depicted later in this chapter is a useful tool for designing or troubleshooting expectations, resources, feedback, and consequences for all performers so they directly and properly—perhaps even synergistically—support established process requirements. Process requirements then link back to macro-level context or marketplace results.

Systematic Performance Analysis: Basic Premises for Success

Consider the following basic premises:

- Any organization can be viewed as existing for the purpose of creating some product(s) or service(s).

- Most organizations are interested in surviving into the future.

- You cannot manage something or control its success if you can't measure it.
- The only practical source for developing measurement standards or criteria is the customer marketplace.
- There is significant opportunity to improve organization performance by clarifying and managing the customer-supplier relationships that join the component parts (internal functions) of any company.

If you agree with these premises, consider the graphically anchored description of a performance analysis model depicted in figures 3-1 through 3-6.

Organization Maps: An Effective Performance Analysis Tool

The analysis process can be described rather simply and succinctly in the model above. However, completing this analysis, documenting your findings, and developing and presenting related recommendations are not quite so straightforward without the use of an extremely valuable tool, organization mapping. An organization map is a graphic representation of how something works. The "something" can be the whole organization in the context of its marketplace or a department or function as it interacts with both internal and external customers and suppliers. The next sections discuss the two general types of organization maps.

Relationship Maps

Relationship maps show the products and services produced by the organization as a whole in the context of its marketplace and usually include this same information for various organizational components. Function- or department-level details highlight the internal customer-supplier network.

The example in figure 3-7 is a simplified relationship map that is one in a series of maps created for Friendly Lender, a company that buys, sells, and services residential secondary mortgage loans. The map shows only the relationships that occur when this lender is developing customer relationships with mortgage brokers and correspondents (lenders who, unlike brokers, actually make loans to homeowners with their own funds and later sell them to companies like Friendly Lender).

The map shows the products and services that the focus organization (Friendly Lender) and key functional parts of the organization (such as the sales department) get from and provide to each in the course of doing business and to make a profit. At this macro relationship level, you can already begin to identify issues or questions for further study. Consider this issue identified for Friendly Lender:

> The quality of the portfolio of customers is an important measure for the sales department. However, this measure is not being evaluated. There should also be an emphasis on building a territory/customer profile database that would belong to Friendly Lender and serve to support management decision making. That is, the database should support setting account executive objectives and resource requirements, completing sales account executive territory match, and so forth, in addition to conducting new sales account executive orientation.

It is important to document issues identified at this initial stage of the performance analysis process. Of particular interest are issues such as missing, inappropriate, or conflicting function-level objectives. For example, in the case of Friendly Lender, the sales department is rewarded for generating (purchasing) loans from brokers and correspondents. However, purchased loans are of value only if the homeowner continues to pay the mortgage obligation and if the obligation pays Friendly Lender more than the price paid to the broker or correspondent.

At Friendly Lender, sales account executives are not being evaluated based on the quality (default rate) of their individual purchased loan portfolios. The credit department, on the other hand, often acts very conservatively (from the perspective of the sales department) because it is evaluated on the quality (default rate) of the company's loan portfolio and not at all on the total loan volume. Because the key measures of these two important functions—the sales department and the credit department—are almost directly in conflict, it is important to determine how to manage the interface between them. Ultimately, results (profitability) must be optimized for Friendly Lender, rather than maximizing the measures for either function.

If you focus your analysis solely within one function or the other, you may fail to help Friendly Lender improve its profit performance although you would help your function-level client (either the sales or credit department) improve its function-specific measures.

Figure 3-1. What an organization does.

An organization converts inputs from suppliers (raw materials, labor, energy, and so forth) into products or services for some client within the customer market.

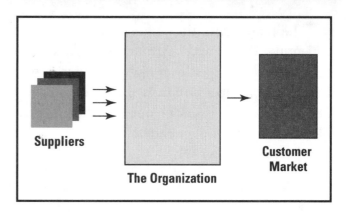

Figure 3-2. An organization adapts to market forces.

An important aspect of this view of the way that organizations operate is that they must be adaptive. They must respond to customer requirements and control their performance using information from both ❶ internal measurements and ❷ external feedback.

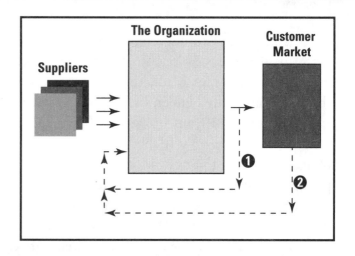

Figure 3-3. A macro view of the organization's functions.

A critical insight is that the components of any organization—the functions—are "wired together" by the products and services they get from and provide to each other in the course of doing business. This macro relationship view must precede detailed process analysis for performance improvement or ongoing goal setting and planning.

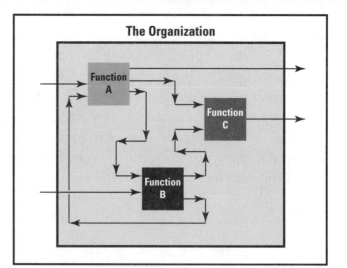

Figure 3-4. View of how an organization really operates.

The traditional way that organizations are organized and managed is functional and vertical as described by the typical organization chart. Performance improvement opportunity and practical, effective management objectives and controls can be identified when an organization is viewed and managed the way that it operates. The "white space"—as Rummler and Brache (1995) call it—between the boxes, or function interfaces, must be specifically addressed to optimize organization performance.

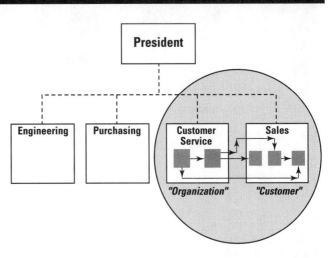

Figure 3-5. Visualizing processes as a series of accomplishments.

Once performance context and relationships have been established, key processes ❶ should be defined to move toward implementation. Process articulation must be in the form of a sequence of accomplishments. Processes are the foundation for describing (linking to) function-level ❷ and position accomplishments. The concept of accomplishment as first defined by Gilbert (1978) is critical to the useful specification of process steps as well as related performer position requirements.

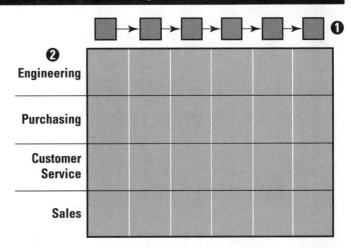

Figure 3-6. Components of the performance environment.

Because people are the organization, it is essential to define accomplishments (expectations) down to the performer/position level. Accomplishments should be linked through processes to organizationally desirable results. Expectations drive the balance of the components of the performance environment and are, therefore, critical. However, all four components must be addressed and managed. It is management's responsibility to provide a supportive performance environment that will facilitate application by performers of relevant skills and knowledge to required job tasks.

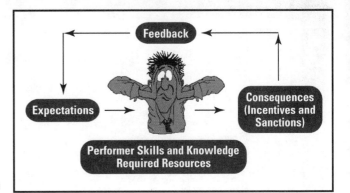

Source: Figures 3-1 through 3-6 reprinted with permission of CMP Associates, 2001.

Figure 3-7. A relationship map for Friendly Lender.

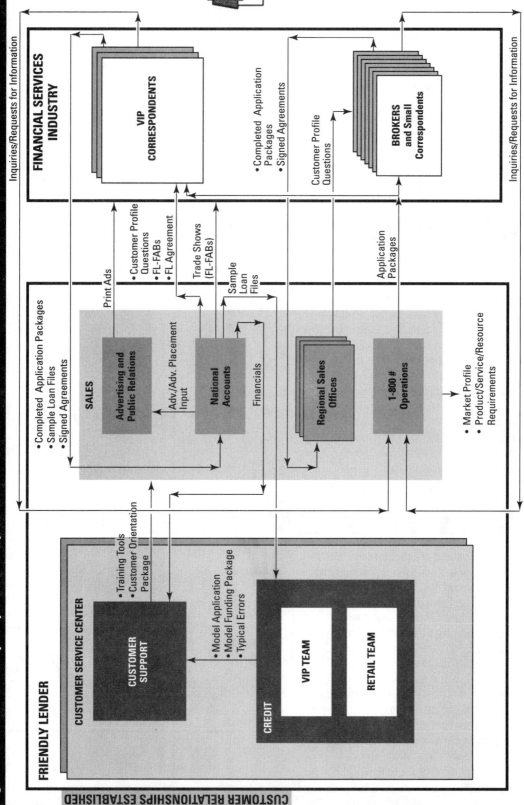

Process Maps

Maps that highlight the flow of steps (accomplishments) required to produce a valued output or to process an important input are process maps.

Figure 3-8 is an example of a very high-level (macro) process map that describes the sequence of accomplishments required to build a portfolio of customers and, thereby, increase loan volume and enhance the bottom line at Friendly Lender. Below the end-to-end process flow is an enlargement of the flow segment that pertains to "customer relationships established." Notice that the steps (shown as boxes) are stated as accomplishments, that is, the things that have to get done rather than what people do.

Be sure that in your zeal to specify accomplishments you don't confuse your client or lose the client's support and understanding. That is, make sure you have identified accomplishments or outcomes, but don't lose important language that performers understand, relate to, and use. For example, "applications screened" is an activity, not an accomplishment. However, it is the language used by performers. In the example in figure 3-8, the performers' language is used in addition to the accomplishment, "customer candidates identified."

Process maps can also identify issues. For example, for the macro step, "customer relationships established," the following issue was revealed:

> How effective account executives are at developing new customers (customer relationships established) depends on the output from the preceding steps in the overall process. There must be a viable "market development planning" subprocess that precedes, and directly supports, the process of establishing *good* customer relationships.

From Macro to Micro: An Analysis Path That Works

Performance analysis must proceed from macro to micro. That is, it is essential to begin with a customer focus that takes into account the context of the marketplace in which the organization, department, or function operates. If you do not begin at the macro level—the relationship and (marketplace) external customer level—you are taking a potentially costly risk. You may identify issues and suggest related improvement opportunities for some important part of the organization at the expense of another part. Such a situation, therefore, may be detrimental to the organization as a whole.

Figure 3-8. A process map for building up a customer portfolio.

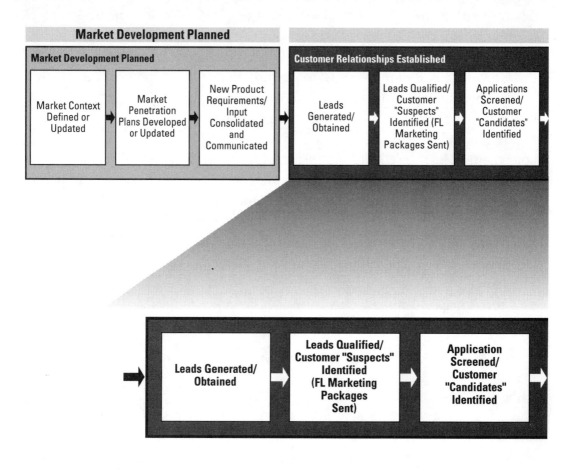

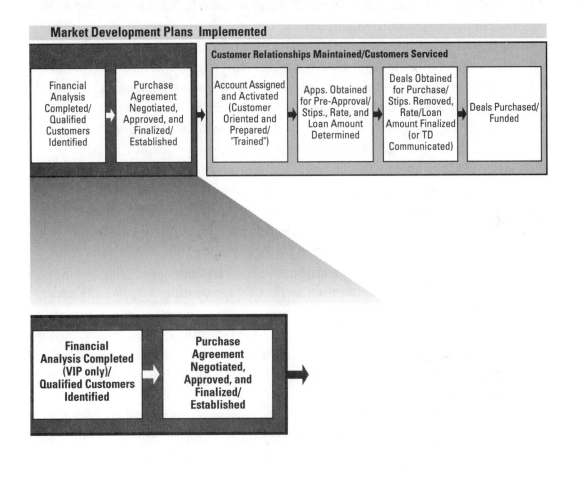

Market Development Plans Implemented

Customer Relationships Maintained/Customers Serviced

| Financial Analysis Completed/ Qualified Customers Identified | Purchase Agreement Negotiated, Approved, and Finalized/ Established | Account Assigned and Activated (Customer Oriented and Prepared/ "Trained") | Apps. Obtained for Pre-Approval/ Stips., Rate, and Loan Amount Determined | Deals Obtained for Purchase/ Stips. Removed, Rate/Loan Amount Finalized (or TD Communicated) | Deals Purchased/ Funded |

Financial Analysis Completed (VIP only)/ Qualified Customers Identified → **Purchase Agreement Negotiated, Approved, and Finalized/ Established**

So you wouldn't want to concentrate exclusively on sales and reward sales account executives for establishing customers (accounts) and generating loans for possible purchase without considering the quality requirements established by the credit function to ensure that business acquired is "good" business with an acceptable (financially anticipated) default rate. By the same token, you wouldn't want credit to reject potentially profitable volume because that function is accountable for default rates/portfolio quality only. If sales volume and revenue are no concern for credit, the result might be lending criteria that are so restrictive as to preclude the company's ability to generate loan volume and make a profit. In this scenario, the loans serviced by Friendly Lender (the company's portfolio) would be perfect with default rates zero or insignificant, but the company would be out of business.

The moral of the story, of course, is that you must start at the macro level, viewing the client organization in the context of its marketplace and defining the internal customer supplier network that supports success with external customers—first. You can't help but identify performance improvement opportunities or questions for further investigation when you complete this macro, context, and relationship-level analyses.

Don't worry if people within the client organization say, "Yes. That's right. Of course, that's the way it works." Such statements mean that you have learned well. People say that they knew the information presented because it makes so much sense now. You've been able to make very complex information and issues so clear and obvious that they think they always knew it worked that way!

What you are doing is building buy-in and ownership by the client for critical performance improvement opportunities and related suggestions or recommendations. Even if you get comments about relationships on your map that are incorrect or missing, view them as opportunities to build buy-in as well. That is, as you enhance and modify your picture (map) to make it more accurate, you are learning, possibly adding to your issues/opportunities, but most important, you are transferring ownership of the analysis results to your client, where it belongs.

Focus on Accomplishments

An accomplishment focus for process specification is the only way that you can build an analysis framework for processes that accurately defines those processes and also remains open to continuous improvement. Outcomes (accomplishments) remain correct and valid almost indefinitely. However, the activities, tools, and techniques used today, no matter how future-oriented or technologically advanced, will be outdated as soon as a new tool is invented, when techniques are changed or streamlined, or when a manual task is automated.

An accomplishment focus is also valuable because it makes process measurement and management very straightforward. Furthermore, accomplishment-based process descriptions provide a framework for the development of process-supportive and performance-based position descriptions. Specifying position requirements by process step (accomplishment) for each function causes the analyst to develop practical, performance-based position descriptions. In fact, when you develop position descriptions based on what is traditional for a function or by starting at the performer level, it is only by sheer luck that positions collectively add up to a company. Figure 3-9 is a graphic representing the use of a process flow to define supporting position requirements.

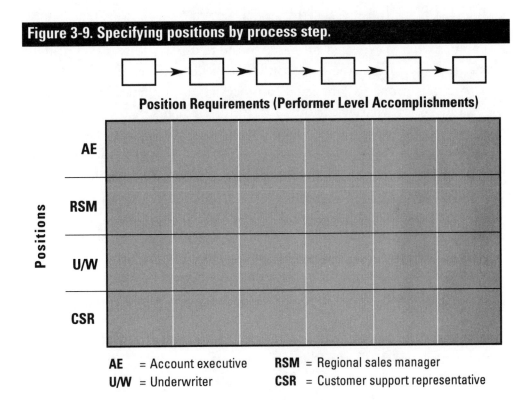

Figure 3-9. Specifying positions by process step.

Position Requirements (Performer Level Accomplishments)

Positions: AE, RSM, U/W, CSR

AE = Account executive   RSM = Regional sales manager
U/W = Underwriter   CSR = Customer support representative

A role matrix, such as figure 3-9, provides a way to identify gaps or overlaps of responsibility as well as issues regarding expectations, resources, consequences, and feedback by process step and position that do or could have an effect on performance. A systematic macro to micro analysis with an accomplishment focus ensures that position descriptions are complete, performance-based, and directly linked, through the processes they support, to organizationally desirable results.

Remember: *People* Are the Organization

It is not enough to use a macro to micro analysis beginning with the external marketplace combined with an accomplishment focus for the specification of process steps and position requirements. People/performers must be specifically addressed because people are the organization. That is, the real estate, the technology, the equipment, and the financial assets are all important. But, without the people, it's not a company and nothing will happen. The best, most progressive ideas will not achieve intended results if the people who must implement and support those ideas are not truly committed.

In addition, management often believes that the one thing that all employees know is what is expected of them. In the first place, this is surprisingly untrue in many organizations. Second, where do these expectations come from? Are they properly connected to processes and organizationally desirable results? And, what about the other three elements of the human performance system—resources, consequences, and feedback?

Table 3-1 is a very simple human performance system model that outlines requirements for each of the four elements (from figure 3-6). It is critical to remember that although all four components are important and must be considered, it is the expectations element that drives the other three. That is, if expectations are not clearly, completely, or correctly (directly linked to and supportive of process steps and valuable organization results) set, nothing will work because expectations drive the human performance system.

As an example of performance analysis at the position level using the HPI model, consider a performer working within the credit function for Friendly Lender. So long as performers are evaluated exclusively on the quality of the portfolio and the default rate, they are not terribly likely to partner with the sales department in taking risks and purchasing loans even when return-on-investment can be negotiated to more than offset (and even anticipate) higher

Table 3-1. Requirements for the four elements of the human performance system as depicted in figure 3-6.

Expectations	Performers should know clearly and up front: What action is desired? When it is required? What are the standards or criteria for success? Performers should have only one task to complete at a time OR a reliable means of prioritizing and selecting between alternatives.
Resources	Performers should be provided with the necessary job skills or learning resources to acquire job skills. Performers should be provided with the necessary tools and job aids to optimize efficient application of skills and knowledge to required job tasks.
Consequences	Consequences should support correct/desired performance. There should be an emphasis on positive consequences (incentives). Positive incentives, whether formal or informal, for undesirable performance and negative consequences for desirable performance should be eliminated.
Feedback	Performers should receive adequate information abut their performance and that information should be: Relevant Accurate Timely Frequent (and consistently delivered) Specific

default rates. Also, you can train either of these groups of performers "until you turn blue in the face," but real on-the-job performance is not going to change until performer expectations, resources, consequences, *and* feedback specifically support desired position outcomes.

Some Final Words of Advice

Performance analysis must be customer focused—first and foremost. It must also be conducted systematically from the marketplace down through the levels of the organization. Accomplishments are the key to useful process and position definition. And, last, but probably most important, performers must

Table 3-2. Critical roles in the change process.

Role	Description
Change Sponsor	An individual or group that controls sufficient "political" power or assets and resources to legitimize and support an intended change
Change Agent	An individual or group responsible for implementing or facilitating the specifics of the change
Change Target	An individual or group that must operate differently, i.e., change

be specifically addressed if you expect performance improvement recommendations to actually be implemented and implemented successfully, no matter how brilliant those recommendations may be.

And, don't forget this last little piece of advice: Throughout any analysis effort, just as during the subsequent implementation of recommendations, any time that you are asking someone to do something differently (no matter how big an improvement it seems to be), you are asking them to change. There is a tremendous inertia around change, and you must keep in mind that there are at least three roles (table 3-2) that must constantly be managed.

So, if your analysis focused on the sales organization turns up a critical dependency on the credit function as well as issues regarding how the relationship is functioning, you may need to seek higher-level sponsorship for your analysis effort. At a minimum, find one or more sponsors within credit.

Your HPI Challenge

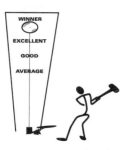

As you embark upon your own performance analyses, consider these questions based on this chapter.

✓ What should be included in the marketplace/context and relationship view of any organization? What is the best way to do a reality check and optimize the usefulness of this view of the organization? What are the risks of skipping this step in your analysis?

_____

_____

_____

_____

_____

✓ What is an accomplishment? Why is it important to specify each process as a sequence of accomplishments versus behaviors or just "stuff"?

_____

_____

✓ What is the human performance system and how is it useful as a part of a systematic performance analysis effort? What are the risks of skipping this step in your analysis?

_____

_____

_____

_____

✓ What is organization mapping, and what makes it a useful tool for performance analysis?

_____

_____

✓ Why is it valuable to get client comments and modifications or enhancements on any maps and issue statements you develop? What do you risk by not soliciting and incorporating enhancements from your client?

_____

_____

_____

_____

✓ What are the various roles in the change process? Why is it important to continue to look at and manage the execution of all three critical roles throughout the entire analysis process?

_____

_____

_____

_____

_____

References

Gilbert, T.F. (1978). *Human Competence: Engineering Worthy Performance.* New York: McGraw-Hill.

Rummler, G.A., and A.P. Brache. (1995). *Improving Performance: How to Manage the White Space on the Organization Chart* (2d edition). San Francisco: Jossey-Bass.

Additional Resources

James, R.I. (1990). *The No-Nonsense Guide to Common Sense Management.* Orangevale, CA: James and Associates.

Panza, C.M. (1989). *Picture This... Your Function, Your Company.* Morristown, NJ: CMP Associates.

Senge, P.M. (1990). *The Fifth Discipline: The Art and Practice of the Learning Organization.* New York: Doubleday/Currency.

About the Author

Carol Panza is a management consultant specializing in performance effectiveness systems for clients in a broad range of industries and functions. As president of her firm, CMP Associates, she is responsible for the success of a broad range of consulting assignments that have taken her to more than 10 countries (so far). Panza is the author of 10 published articles and chapters in four books on performance topics as well as her own book first published by CMP Associates in 1989 entitled *Picture This... Your Function, Your Company.*

Gap Analysis: The Path From Today's Performance Reality to Tomorrow's Performance Dreams

Martha Boyd

Key Points

> The difference between the beginning point, or current performance level, and the endpoint, or desired performance level, is the performance gap.

> The identification and definition of the performance gap is a critical step in helping an organization address performance improvement needs.

> Gap analysis ties together all of the performance issues and forms the basis for the next steps in the process—the identification of causes and the selection of interventions.

> In gap analysis, the problem is reframed into current behaviors and expected outcomes.

> Performance gaps can represent performance levels that are lower than expected, levels that meet expectations, or levels that exceed expectations.

In this age of fast-moving change and fierce competition, the most crucial challenge to improving productivity comes not in the form of upgrading equipment or of having the "latest and greatest" but in the development of an organization's most critical resource, its employees.

The HPI practitioner's focus is on improving human performance. Before you, the practitioner, can focus on the journey to improving performance, you must first define two things: the beginning point, or current performance level, and the endpoint, or desired performance level. The difference between these two points is referred to as the gap. Defining and measuring that difference is called gap analysis. This chapter focuses on the following:

- the role of gap analysis in HPI
- how to conduct a gap analysis
- critical issues in gap analysis.

Analyzing the Analyses

To ensure some degree of clarity in communication, it is good practice to define a few important terms. The following terms specifically differentiate gap analysis from the other types of analyses that are performed by HPI practitioners:

- Business analysis—the first step in the HPI model—examines the organization's mission, vision, values, goals, and strategies.

- Performance analysis identifies and clarifies the problem or performance gap by focusing on three areas: desired performance state, actual performance state, and the gap between desired and actual performance. The purpose of this analysis is not to point out problems, but rather to identify factors in the environment that support performance improvement. The second stage of the HPI model encompasses this type of analysis.

- Gap analysis describes the difference between current results and consequences and desired results and consequences. It ties together all of the performance issues and forms the basis for the next steps in the process, the identification of causes, and the selection of interventions. Gap analysis is part of performance analysis, the second stage of the HPI model.

- Cause analysis determines why the performance gap exists and identifies the factors contributing to the gap. These activities occur in the third stage of the HPI model.

The Role of Gap Analysis in HPI

To make sense of gap analysis you need to understand the part it plays in HPI. Human performance improvement is based on the premise that there is a need for improvement or, more specifically, that there is dissimilarity between what is actually happening and what you want to happen. Many models have been developed to represent and to help explain the process of gap analysis.

As you know, HPI is a comprehensive strategy incorporating a set of methods or processes by which information is gathered (figure 1-2). This information is used to develop interventions that provide effective, economical, and practical solutions to performance problems. Gap analysis is a critical activity carried out during the second stage of the HPI model—performance analysis. During this stage, organizational expectations are defined, and the performance gap is identified.

The identification and definition of the performance gap is a critical step in helping an organization address HPI. Within the HPI model, the performance analysis has two distinct purposes: to identify organizational performance goals and objectives, and to pursue information about factors that influence performance, either hindering or encouraging improvement.

The practitioner starts by identifying the organization's standards and expectations. Performance improvement is based on the premise that there is a gap between what is actually happening and what is embodied by the organization's standards and expectations. The outcome of performance analysis is the identification and measurement of the performance gap.

How to Conduct a Gap Analysis

The overall performance of an organization is measured by how well it meets the expectations of its customers. If the customer is not satisfied the first question is "Why?" If you don't know what the problem is, you won't know how to find the solution. To find the right solution—one that will solve the problem, address the performance gap, and meet customer's expectations—you must identify the discrepancy between actual and preferred performance levels. Your aim is to discover and define the discrepancy. You are the detective!

Table 4-1. The *do*s and *don't*s of gap analysis.

*Do*s	*Don't*s
• Do ask clarifying questions: *why* questions.	• Don't start out by proposing an answer; you don't know what the problem is.
• Do ask specific questions: *who, what, how* questions.	• Don't assume the customer knows what the problem is.
• Do listen for what is said about what isn't being done.	• Don't get sidetracked into placing blame.
• Do determine who the customer is and what he or she wants done.	

To help you keep the proper focus for the analysis, it's important to keep a few guidelines in mind when starting out (table 4-1).

Human performance improvement uses a systematic approach to performance gap analysis. This approach consists of a series of sequential steps represented by inquiries into the areas where performance is an issue. Your analysis should gather information about the following:

- Is there a problem?
- What are the demonstrations or manifestations of the problem?
- What is the problem?
- How important is the problem?

The critical outcome is the identification of a performance gap. This can be done using a single investigator or with a group or team. The procedure used to gather information includes reviewing documents and records to learn about present levels of performance and functioning, as well as anticipated directions for the organization. You can also use various techniques to gather information about thoughts and impressions.

Interviews, surveys, focus groups, and corrective action reports are all proven means of collecting data. The choice of organizational research method depends on the size of the targeted performance group and the size of the group affected by the performance. The important thing to remember is to get to the root of the matter. What performance is the real issue?

Important Questions to Identify and Prioritize Gaps

The systemic approach to analyzing performance gaps includes two areas of inquiry. The first area of inquiry is to identify the gaps:

- Who is the customer, or who is affected by the performance issue?
- Whose performance is the problem?
- Why does the customer think there is a problem?
- What is the actual performance level?
- What is the desired performance level?

The second area of inquiry is to determine the priority of the gaps:

- How important is the identified gap?
- How often does the gap occur?
- How costly will it be to resolve the gap?

Case Study: Commercial Printing Company

The following case study is based on a preliminary consultation with the training and supervisory team for the advertising insert division of Oz Publications. (References to commercial names and organizational trademarks have been changed to protect the confidentiality of the client.)

The Situation. Oz Publications designs and produces advertisement inserts for distribution in a local daily newspaper. The company has developed a proprietary method for product layout using a template that allows graphics and lettering to be imported into a single template. This process is complicated and requires the assembly individual to import electronically the elements of the flyer from other departments. The photo and text components are imported into a template and then sent on to a series of quality control editors. Each component is developed using a different software application. Figure 4-1 shows the various process flows and how they should work together to create Oz's advertising.

The digital division supervisor received complaints from the quality control editors about high error rates. According to the reports from editing, the final mock-ups and prints contained multiple errors. The complaints included the following:

- improper linking of photography files
- improper formatting of text
- errors in import and export of files.

Up to 65 percent of the mock-ups and prints had to be reworked because of text errors and 45 percent required rework for digital errors. Table 4-2

Figure 4-1. Workflow chart for Oz Publications.

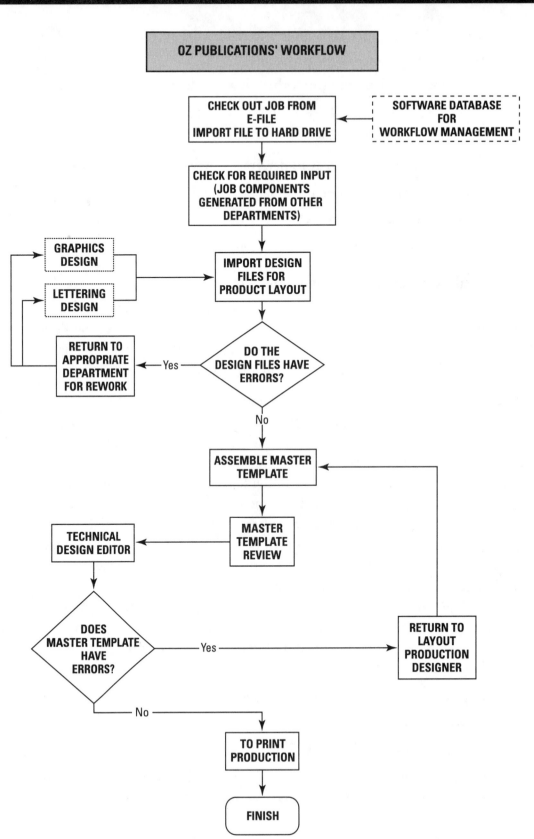

Table 4-2. Breakdown of errors encountered by the technical design editors and layout production designers from September through November.

Error Type	Number of Errors	Percent of Total
Incorrect file name	21	10.5%
Graphic information missing	13	6.5%
File(s) missing	19	9.5%
Delegated incorrectly to proofreading	4	2.0%
Incorrect parameters	23	11.5%
Improper templates, etc.	2	1.0%
File inaccessible	32	16.0%
File too large	1	0.5%
Font error	41	20.5%
Incorrectly linked layers	36	18.5%
Locked layers	8	4.0%
Total Errors	**200**	**100%**

reveals the high error rates that occurred during a three-month period. These errors were costly in terms of time and effort for rework. The clients were none too pleased either when errors got past the editors and appeared in the published inserts. Clearly, action was needed.

Initially, the organization defined the problem in terms of training needs. Over the prior eight months, the entire workforce in the photo and lettering departments received three two-day training sessions on digital workflow. Digital workflow sessions included training on software applications, technical execution, and design interface. At the completion of the digital workflow training, the error rates were again measured. Unfortunately, they had not changed. So, what was the problem at Oz?

Gap Analysis. The director of training contacted external performance consultants. An initial meeting was set up with the director of training, the trainers for digital software, production supervisors for both the photo and lettering departments, and the performance specialists. The consultants observed a digital training session and interviewed the editing staff for the photo and lettering departments. Interviews were conducted with the product assemblers about their opinions on digital training. The performance consultants collected data on the rework error rates and types of errors that cropped up.

The production quality standards of the organization were based upon the following criteria that defined acceptable performance levels:

- rework error rate less than 15 percent on final-phase editing
- rework rates for initial proofreading less than 30 percent
- file import procedures followed correctly in 75% of jobs.

Results of the Gap Analysis. Observation of the digital workflow training sessions showed that although the instructors were very knowledgeable about the subject content, the content was not well organized and the presentation was not smooth. The following observations were based on training session observations and interviews with training participants:

- course content was covered at a rapid pace
- training session content did not follow the course workbook
- importance of error rate control was not emphasized in training
- time for trainee questions was minimal
- trainees had varying levels of software knowledge and expertise
- job aids and work instructions were not available for reference on the job.

The performance consultants sent a gap analysis report to the director of training and the production supervisor. The report included a general summary of findings and initial recommendations. It suggested that three major performance gaps were affecting the work quality:

1. Training personnel assumed that all the participants had the necessary software knowledge and skill levels to complete the training successfully.

2. The trainees were not retaining the course content and, therefore, were unable to transfer the skills from training to the job.

3. The trainers lacked necessary teaching and organizational skills.

So, What Happened?

The management at Oz Publications agreed to make some changes. Training in digital software applications was offered to the product assemblers

---

Gap Analysis Quick Check

- Analyze observable workplace behavior.
- Reframe problem in terms of current behaviors.
- Reframe problem into expected outcomes.
- Ask questions that will define the importance of the discrepancy.

---

before digital workflow training. The training staff developed a digital work-flow instructor's guide based on the workbook. The instructor's guide included detailed lesson plans for each session. A series of easy-to-follow, quick-reference job aids were developed for digital workflow processes.

Critical Issues in Gap Analysis

More often than not, organizations approach problem solving with the "solution" already in hand. If the solution is the correct one, great, but usually you find you have a great solution to a problem that is not yours. You must ask the right questions of the right people concerning the right issues.

As this chapter has shown, the most important challenge in performance improvement analysis is to define the gap properly. Performance gaps are not always defined by deficiencies; sometimes they represent competency. Performance gaps can represent performance levels that are less than is expected, levels that meet expectations, or levels that exceed expectations. Gaps can be seen as opportunities to improve competency levels through remedial interventions or opportunities to excel through increased competency.

Your HPI Challenge

To develop a successful solution, you must have a clear description of the problem. Gap analysis develops congruence between the "what is," or present performance, and the "what is desired," or the stated performance goal of the organization. Now, it's time to apply your new learning about gap analysis to some thought problems.

✓ Think about the business goals of your organization. Are they in alignment with the "what is" situation? If not, what research tools could you apply to measure the gap? What questions might you ask?

_____

_____

_____

_____

✓ Recall the case study. How was competency a problem in the case study presented? Can you think of a similar situation in your organization?

_____

_____

_____

_____

✓ How can too much competency lead to a performance gap? Have you observed this in your organization? What measures could you apply to assess the performance gap?

_____

_____

_____

_____

_____

Additional Resources

Dean, P.J., and D.E. Ripley (editors). (1998). *Performance Improvement Interventions: Performance Technologies in the Workplace.* Washington: International Society for Performance Improvement.

Hale, J. (1998). *The Performance Consultant's Fieldbook: Tools and Techniques for Improving Organizations and People.* San Francisco: Jossey-Bass/Pfeiffer.

Langdon, D.G., K.S. Whiteside, and M.M. McKenna (editors). (1999). *Intervention Resource Guide: 50 Performance Improvement Tools.* San Francisco: Jossey-Bass/Pfeiffer.

Mager, R.F., and P. Pipe. (1984). *Analyzing Performance Problems: Or You Really Oughta Wanna* (2d edition). Belmont, CA: David S. Lake Publishers.

Robinson, D.G., and J.C. Robinson. (1998). *Moving from Training to Performance: A Practical Guidebook.* San Francisco: Berrett-Koehler.

Swanson, J.A. (1994). *Analysis for Improving Performance: Tools for Diagnosing Organizations and Documenting Workplace Expertise.* San Francisco: Berrett-Koehler.

Van Tiem, D.M., J.L. Moseley, and J.C. Dessinger. (2000). *Fundamentals of Performance Technology: A Guide to Improving People, Process, and Performance.* Washington: International Society for Performance Improvement.

About the Author

Martha Boyd has been a performance consultant with the Business and Technical Center of the Metropolitan Community Colleges of Kansas City, Missouri, for five years. She has worked six years in postsecondary education student services as a specialist in student development. Previous to her work as a performance consultant, she spent eight years as a member of a treatment team for a large metropolitan mental health hospital. Her primary area was vocational development and assessment.

Her educational background is in educational psychology and research, and counselor education and development. She received a bachelor of arts degree in psychology from the University of Kansas and a master of science degree in counseling psychology from the University of Kansas. Boyd is also a licensed professional counselor. She anticipates receiving a doctorate in education with an emphasis in counselor development and family therapy from Kansas State University in July 2002.

Cause Analysis—Don't Assume Training Is the Answer, Don't Assume Anything!

George M. Piskurich

Key Points

- Training is just one possible answer to a performance gap.
- The difference between optimal and actual is the performance gap.
- Your basic question is: "Why does the performance gap exist?"
- There are a number of systematic methods you can use for determining causes.
- Try to create levels or classes of causes.

Using the HPI model (figure 1-2) you have determined business goals, the desired performance state, and the gap between this state and the current reality of the business. At this point (and sometimes well before) someone often decides that because a performance gap exists, some training is necessary. To conduct the "required" training, trainers, training consultants, subject matter experts, or another person is brought in to create and deliver a training program. This approach works very well unless the cause of the performance gap is something that cannot be addressed by training. If such is the case—and it often is—then this approach works very badly, or not at all.

The Danger Inherent in Assumptions

Suppose you find that production is below average on a particular assembly line and needs to be brought up to standard if the company is going to make its productivity and profit goals. One of your options is to assume that the assembly line workers don't know how to do their jobs properly and, therefore, that training is the answer for this performance gap.

Another option, however, is to dig a bit deeper into the problem and find that the real cause is a high number of replacement workers on this particular line, so it is obvious that you just need to train them.

Or, you may dig just a bit more and find that the reason there are so many replacement workers is that many hand injuries occur on this assembly line, causing workers to take time off the job. This situation doesn't seem to call for a training intervention, but further analysis shows that the reason for so many hand injuries is that the workers are not using the hand guard that should be attached to each machine.

Now you have a real training issue: instructing workers as to the importance of hand guards, unless, of course, the hand guards aren't being used because they are not available, or don't function well, or interfere with the work so much that they have been removed from the machines.

The moral of this story is that in HPI you should not assume that a performance gap indicates a need for training, in fact, you should try not to assume anything. For HPI, cause analysis is used to determine why the performance gap exists and identify the factors that are contributing to it. This process allows the HPI practitioner to choose the most effective intervention to close the performance gap.

What You Need to Know and Do

- You need to KNOW how to define the concept of a cause analysis.
- You need to UNDERSTAND the purpose of a cause analysis.
- You need to KNOW how to place cause analysis into the HPI structure.
- You need to CREATE your own job aid for performing a cause analysis.

Causes of Performance Gaps

The cause behind a performance gap may be lack of training, or it may be any of the following:

- a lack of knowledge or skills on the part of the workers, which probably does indicate the need for a training program but might just as easily be corrected by a job aid or performance support tool
- a lack of the proper physical resources to do the job, which likely necessitates some changes in the work process
- a problem or weak link in the structure or process of the work or work flow
- a need for more information concerning the job, which may look like a training need but just as often emanates from modification of company objectives, management miscommunication, or a need for documentation
- a lack of or a change in leadership
- lack of information about the consequences of poorly done work for the organization or personally for the performer
- a problem with the motives and expectations of the workforce
- inadequate feedback
- inadequate incentives or rewards
- performer's lack of capacity to do the job because of a hiring, selection, or promotion problem.

One View of the Problem

In the case of the below-average assembly line discussed previously, one possible cause for the performance gap may be a lack of feedback to performers concerning the adequacy of their work. Optimally, performers should receive feedback every day. You find through your cause analysis that there is a quality meeting once a week. Although this frequency isn't optimal, interviews with the workers indicate that the difference is not significant, so you reject your hypothesis that lack of feedback is a cause.

Another View of the Problem

You may believe from analyzing your preliminary data that the problem is really one of worker capacity. You find that optimally all assembly line workers should have a high school diploma, but that 30 percent do not. Further investigation reveals that proper maintenance of the machines requires workers to read at an eighth-grade level, which the 30 percent nongraduates (and even some of the graduates) cannot. As improper maintenance can reduce machine output by as much as 25 percent, you have probably found a significant cause for the performance gap. Further analysis finds that almost a quarter of the machines did not receive proper maintenance during your observation period. This finding heightens your suspicion that you have isolated a cause of the gap.

Methods for Performing Cause Analysis

When performing a cause analysis, the three things you need to determine for these, or any other suspected causes of the performance gap, are:

- What is optimal for this aspect?
- What is actual for the company?
- Is this difference enough to cause the performance gap?

Stated in its simplest terms, the question you want to answer in your cause analysis is: Why does the performance gap exist? You know that there is a problem as you've done a performance analysis, and you even know what it is as you've done an effective gap analysis, but the cause analysis helps you determine why it is. Basically, the cause analysis stops you from doing the wrong things for the right reason.

A Tried and True Example

A classic example of this process at work is the company that had a problem (call it a performance gap) with new product sales. Although the old products were selling well, none of the new introductions were living up to expectations. The obvious cause was that the salespeople just didn't understand the advantages of the new products.

A number of expensive training programs later, new product sales were still lower than expected, as were old product sales because the salespeople were spending their time training instead of selling.

A cause analysis found that the incentives for selling a new product in terms of bonus and special prizes were exactly the same as the ones for selling old products. This reward system seemed fair until discussions with the salesforce revealed that it took them almost five times longer to introduce a new product to a customer as it did to resell them on an old one. As for the new customers that the new products were expected to bring in, forget it! "I can sell $3,000 worth of our basic line to an old customer in the time it takes me to just introduce myself to a new customer," said the company's most successful salesperson (an exemplary performer).

So, what was the true cause behind the lagging sales of new products? A poorly planned incentive system was the culprit. The intervention that was based on this knowledge changed the incentive program, and raised new product sales dramatically.

Asking the right people the right questions is certainly an accepted method of cause analysis, but the causes are seldom as clear as in this example. You often need to use a more systematic method of cause analysis such as structured brainstorming, fishbone diagrams, and the five *whys*.

Structured Brainstorming

In brainstorming, the idea is to come up with as many ideas as possible and then whittle them down to a couple that seem the most promising. There is no limit to the number of people you can involve in a session, but the group size becomes unwieldy if you have more than four or five people without creating subgroups. Make sure that your participants have enough knowledge concerning the problem at hand to provide reasonable input. Get to the best ideas through any process that is reasonable for your group: voting, consensus discussion, or validation by a third party.

The basic agenda for a brainstorming session includes the following steps:

1. Agree on the central question.
2. Have each member offer one idea.
3. Record suggestions.
4. Go back and generate all ideas that relate to each suggestion.
5. Review the total list for clarity and duplication.

Fishbone Diagrams

These pictures graphically display in increasing detail possible causes related to a problem. They are best used for preliminary work in cause analysis. There are various formats, such as the ones shown in figures 5-1 and 5-2. However, use them with care as they sometimes isolate symptoms rather than causes.

The Five *Whys*

This popular technique tends to tell the story of causes and effects starting from back to front. It gives you more depth and is useful with more complex problems or for performance gaps that stem from multiple or contributing causes. It basically works like this:

1. Write down the problem.

2. Ask and answer the question, "Why does this happen?"

3. Turn each answer into the next *why* question.

4. Repeat for five iterations.

5. Keep track of relationships between cause statements and next level of *why*.

Other Methods

Other ways to establish causes are found in the root cause analysis methodologies that are basic to most quality control processes. These techniques include affinity diagrams, Pareto charts, scatter diagrams, and other quality techniques, such as those in Brassard's 1996 *The Memory Jogger Plus.*

You can also use many of the same analytical methods for cause analysis that you use for other analyses. These include

- surveys (telephone, written, or Internet)
- interviews with key workers with follow-up observation
- simulated demonstrations or live observations, or both
- panels
- reviews of performance data
- interviews of deficient performers and their supervisors or managers
- reviews of records such as performance appraisals, HR records, disciplinary actions, lost time histories, maintenance records, and so forth.

You'll need to develop some foundation skills for these methods. You must be a good listener, a fast writer (or proficient audiotape operator), a careful reader, a good summarizer, and a competent developer of both open-ended

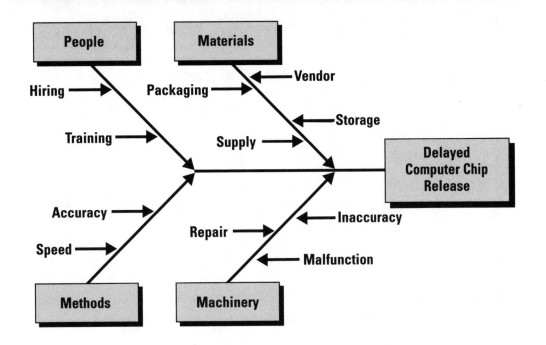

Figure 5-1. Example of a fishbone diagram used for cause analysis.

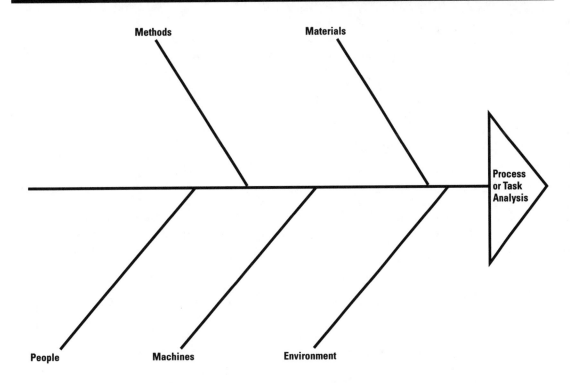

Figure 5-2. Another example of a fishbone diagram used for cause analysis.

Some Web Resources for Cause Analysis Methods

Fishbone Diagrams
- http://web.mit.edu/tqm/cause_effect.html
- http://courses.bus.ualberta.ca/orga432-reshef/fishbone.html

Brainstorming
- http://www.graphic.org/brainst.html
- http://www.mindtools.com/brainstm.html
- http://www.fastcompany.com/change/change_feature/kelley.html

Five *Whys*
- http://www.qaproject.org/pdf/part2.pdf

Affinity Diagrams and Other QC Methods
- http://www.skymark.com/resources/tools/affinity_diagram.asp
- http://www.usbr.gov/guide/toolbox/affinity.htm
- http://thequalityportal.com/mix/q_affinity.htm
- http://www.goalqpc.com/RESEARCH/MJII/MJSELCHT.html
- http://akao.larc.nasa.gov/dfc/tqc.html

and closed-ended questions. Here are a few more hints you might find useful when using these methods:

- *Focus your questions by asking:* "When the problem occurs, where does it occur?" "How do you monitor the problem?
- *Always ask for more information:* "Am I asking the right questions?" "Did I miss anything?" "What are you surprised that I did not ask about?" "Is there anyone else with whom I should speak?" "Are there other potential causes that the survey didn't ask about?"
- *Create a focused survey:* Give respondents a list of potential causes and ask which ones they think contribute to the problem.

Validate your causes through direct observation. Remember that this form of data gathering can be suspect if the employees know someone is watching changes their behavior. The Hawthorne effect and the Heisenberg uncertainty principle may come into play. Also, although direct observation is often the best method, it usually takes the most time.

Levels of Causes

To make the determination of causes for a performance gap somewhat easier to get your arms around, it is often useful to consider causes in terms of levels or classes. A good test of the completeness of your cause analysis is to check each performance gap against the listed levels or classes to make sure you've considered all possible causes. Here are two common example structures that you might use:

Example 1

- *Organizational:* Mission, policies and procedures, organizational structure
- *Management/Process:* Poor communications by management, wrong incentives
- *Job performer:* Motivation, capacity, confidence
- *Skills and knowledge:* Knowledge, resources, tools
- *Environmental:* Job demands, time, lack of consequences.

Example 2

- *Information:* Unclear expected performance; poor work instructions; limited feedback
- *Resources:* Tools, people, time
- *Incentives:* Financial, nonfinancial, developmental, negative consequences
- *Knowledge and skills:* Training
- *Capacity:* Selection, people/position match
- *Motives:* Work incentives.

Some "Look For" Statements to Guide You

You may have realized by now that determining causes is not as simple as it might seem at first. The example classifications cover a wide range of possibilities, and the methods mentioned earlier can be difficult for the inexperienced practitioner to handle properly. To help you along, refer to the series of "look for" statements provided in table 5-1 when you do a cause analysis. These should help you to gather the data you need to isolate the right causes of your performance gap.

You will see that yet another classification scheme was used for the "look for" statements, and you may note that there is some overlap among classes. You can create your own personal job aid by classifying the "look for" statements in a way that is logical for yourself, in whatever structure works best for you. It's your job aid so change the "look for" statements and their classification in any way you like.

Obviously you can't use all these "look for" statements every time you are doing a cause analysis, but taken as a group they should help you to remember what you need to be looking for in terms of causes of the performance gap. The most important thing is that you proceed with a cause analysis before deciding on an intervention to close the performance gap. How you carry out the cause analysis is largely up to you.

The Case of the Rejected Farkels

The following case study should help you to understand the possible depth (and time) needed to do cause analysis and to see some of the causes of a performance gap that could go unnoticed if a cause analysis is not performed adequately.

A manufacturing organization was having a problem with the number of rejected items coming off the assembly lines. To protect the innocent, let's call them farkels. If the farkel was rejected during final inspection, it was declared a total loss. The item was sent to the dump where it might be recycled as raw material or simply stored indefinitely. All the work that went into assembling it was lost, as was profit from its sale, the cost of the material, and the cost of paying the dump to dispose of the rejected pieces. These costs made rejected farkels very expensive.

The performance problem here is readily observable, there are too many substandard farkels coming from the assembly lines. Some organizations would have considered this a skills and knowledge problem and created a training program on reducing rejected farkels. This organization, however, decided to bring in a team of performance consultants to do cause analysis on the performance problem.

Table 5-1. List of "look for" statements to consider in cause analysis.

Market/Organizational Level	Management Level	Process/Function Level	Job Performer Level
☐ Look for recent changes that occurred in the company	☐ Look for disincentives that affect achieving the proper performance	☐ Look for new procedures recently put in place	☐ Look for trends (up or down) in work quality
☐ Look for trends (up or down) in the company	☐ Look for a lack of confidence in the workers' ability to do job on the part of managers	☐ Look for new systems or equipment	☐ Look to see if all performers doing the same task have same problem
☐ Look to see if the gap is isolated within one group or is common throughout the organization	☐ Look for disagreements between managers and workers as to job values	☐ Look to see if work processes are optimally organized	☐ Look for job function changes
☐ Look for new products or services that have been recently implemented	☐ Look at where authority resides compared to where responsibility is placed	☐ Look to see if the physical environment is conducive to high level performance	☐ Look for changes in behaviors of workers or groups
☐ Look at the current business environment (competitors, product age, etc.)	☐ Look at management's responsiveness to worker needs and complaints	☐ Look at work group priorities and their consistency with performance measures	☐ Look for a lack of confidence in ability to do the job on the part of the workers
☐ Look for reorganization, consolidation, or merger	☐ Look to see if the right people are being recruited and hired	☐ Look at communications both up and down the line	☐ Look to see if the workers are given enough data and information to do job properly
☐ Look to see if the organization's mission or vision has changed	☐ Look to see if feedback is timely and sufficient	☐ Look for job aids	☐ Look for conflicting job demands
☐ Look to see if the organizational structure has recently changed	☐ Look for goals being communicated to all levels	☐ Look at materials consumed during performance, their availability and quality	☐ Look to see if performers have sufficient time to do job properly
☐ Look to see if cultural values or norms are changing in the organization or workforce	☐ Look at regular versus special incentives	☐ Look at staffing levels and staffing requirements	☐ Look for barriers to performance and their sources
☐ Look for restrictive policies that inhibit worker or organizational performance	☐ Look for compensation commensurate with performance	☐ Look for tasks that interfere with each other	☐ Compare high and low performers
☐ Look at the organizational climate	☐ Look at how management perceives training programs	☐ Look for tasks that are boring or socially negative	☐ Look at master (exemplary) performers
		☐ Look for safety issues that affect performance	☐ Look at job standards and their reasonableness
			☐ Look for clear, personal consequences of poor performance
			☐ Look to see if incentives are appropriate

(continued next page)

Table 5-1. List of "look for" statements to consider in cause analysis. *(continued)*

Market/Organizational Level	Management Level	Process/Function Level	Job Performer Level
☐ Look for linkages between performance and organizational goals ☐ Look at and listen to corporate history	☐ Look at management's expectations for training	☐ Look at how training is matched to performance ☐ Look at what is covered in training programs ☐ Look at the tools and equipment needed to do job ☐ Look at job instructions for clarity and completeness ☐ Look to see if job instructions are followed	☐ Look to see if the workers want to achieve the expected results ☐ Look to see what the workers expect for top performance ☐ Look to see if performers agree with the way the task is supposed to be done ☐ Look for tools and materials that are not ergonomically sound ☐ Look for links to another performer's deficient output ☐ Look for high turnover and find out why ☐ Look at turnover and promotion histories ☐ Look at how learners perceive training ☐ Look for adequate time for training

Data Gathering

The team initiated its analysis by requesting a demonstration of how farkels were made. With this knowledge in hand, the consultants held a series of interviews with assembly line workers, supervisors, managers, and quality control specialists. Each worker interview was followed by an observation of that worker making farkels. Both underachieving and exemplary performers were interviewed and observed.

Information uncovered in these interviews and observations led to another series of interviews, this time with farkel engineers, machine maintenance technicians and their supervisors, and raw material handlers and their supervisors.

After these processes were analyzed, plant management was interviewed, and another series of observations of farkel construction on various lines was carried out.

The Cause Analysis

In the cause analysis report, the team reported that training was indeed a causative factor in scrapped farkels. The training was erratic, done by operators who were on light duty and not necessarily trained or equipped to be trainers. They did not follow the training design that had been created by someone some time ago. (No one was quite sure who or when, but it was a good design if followed properly.)

They also found other causes:

- *Use of substandard raw material at the front end of the assembly line:* This was not due to the specifications being inadequate, but to management decisions to use the "out-of-spec" materials because no others were available. The line had to make farkels to meet the target productivity for the shift. In addition, the assembly line operators began to question why they had standards at all, and if other standards could be ignored too.

- *An emphasis on quantity not quality:* All plant goals were stated in terms of farkels made, not how many were actually able to be sold to the consumer. In fact, the operator who was considered tops in the plant earned that reputation (and an award) by holding the record for producing the most farkels in one shift. When asked how many of those were rejected, he said he didn't know. Finally, management bonuses were related to number of farkels produced, not necessarily shipped.

- *Lack of communication:* Though the data was available and had even been distributed for a time, no operator currently knew how many rejected farkels had been produced on each shift or the overall number for the plant. No time was allowed for operators going off shift to talk with the next ones coming on about problems that the machine might be having.

- *Inadequate policies and procedures:* Though the machines on the line required constant calibration, the operators were not permitted to do calibrations. Only mechanics could officially change machine settings, but they were not always available. The operators could choose to wait for a mechanic (thus reducing the number of farkels he made), fix it himself (which was contrary to policy and could lead to trouble with the boss), or simply keep making farkels with a maladjusted machine (which most chose to do).

- *Lack of quality control:* It was also found that there were no procedures that set quality control standards at the end of the line. This meant that each quality control technician decided which farkels passed and which did not based on his own judgment. Often farkels that were rejected by one technician were held back by the line supervisor until another technician clocked in who then passed them.

- *Promotion policies:* The team found that promotion was based on longevity, not skill. Therefore, being the best machine operator (or even the fastest) had no motivational incentive. This policy led to workers being promoted to operator positions or to more complex machines without the skills necessary to do the job properly. Training was inadequate for new hires, but it was practically nonexistent for promoted workers.

- *Environmental causes:* Job performers faced myriad environmental challenges on the job. For example, different types of machines fell under a single job classification so operators were sometimes assigned to machines that they were not very familiar with. A laser guide was difficult to see when the machine's lights were on, and a critical cutting tool would not remain sharp. The old hands taught a procedural short cut to new hires even though they were not yet capable of using the technique properly.

You may have noticed that the team found causes in all the different categories mentioned earlier. A cynical person might observe that this is a fictional case because there were so many obvious, perfect causes. However, this cause analysis took the better part of a month by a team of three performance technologists.

Summary

Cause analysis is one of the most difficult yet most critical aspects of the HPI process. It is the link between the performance analysis that defines performance problems and the interventions that make the analysis worth the time and money that was spent on it.

Cause analysis can be very systematic through the use of root cause analysis tools or somewhat more visceral when interviews and observations are used.

Your HPI Challenge

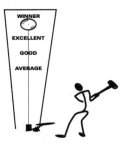

You know the rule: *First* perform a cause analysis, *then* decide on the right intervention. What problems might you face if you don't heed this advice?

_____

_____

_____

_____

_____

_____

_____

_____

✓ Consult some of the Websites listed in the chapter. Which of these methods would likely contribute valuable information for a cause analysis carried out at your organization? Who might you include in a brainstorming session to identify possible causes? Who would you need to interview? Who should receive surveys?

_____

_____

_____

_____

_____

_____

_____

_____

✓ Customize the list of "look for" statements so that the statements fall under categories that are most logical for you. You will find the list to be an invaluable job aid as you embark on cause analyses.

Reference

Brassard, M. (1996). *The Memory Jogger Plus.* Methuen, MA: Goal/QPC.

Additional Resources

Fuller, J., and J. Farrington. (1999). *From Training to Performance Improvement: Navigating the Transition.* San Francisco: Pfeiffer.

Gilbert, T. (1996). *Human Competence: Engineering Worthy Performance.* Washington DC: International Society for Performance Improvement.

Harless, J.H. (1975). *An Ounce of Analysis Is Worth a Pound of Objections.* Newnan, GA: Harless Performance Guild.

Kaufman, R. (1992). *Strategic Planning Plus: An Organizational Guide.* Thousand Oaks, CA: Sage Publications.

Mager, R.F., and P. Pipe. (1984). *Analyzing Performance Problems: Or You Really Oughta Wanna.* Belmont, CA: Pitman.

Rossett, A. (1999). *First Things Fast: A Handbook for Performance Analysis.* San Francisco: Jossey-Bass/Pfeiffer.

Rossett, A. (1990). "Overcoming Obstacles to Needs Assessment." *Training,* *27*(3), 36–41.

Rossett, A. (1987). *Training Needs Assessment.* Englewood Cliffs, NJ: Educational Technology Publications.

Rummler, G.A., and A.P. Brache. (1995). *Performance Improvement: How to Manage the White Space on the Organization Chart* (2d edition). San Francisco: Jossey-Bass.

About the Author

George Piskurich specializes in e-learning design, performance improvement, and telecommuting initiatives. He has more than 20 years of experience as a classroom instructor, instructional designer, and corporate training director, developing classroom, multimedia, and distance learning programs.

Piskurich has presented at 30-plus conferences and symposia including the International Self-Directed Learning Symposium, and the international conferences sponsored by ASTD and the International Society for Performance Improvement.

Among his publications are books on learning technology, self-directed learning, and telecommuting. He has edited books on instructional technology, HPI, and e-learning and written journal articles and book chapters on various topics. He can be reached at gpiskurich@cs.com or his Website, gpiskurich.com.

Selecting an HPI Project: Finding an Early, Manageable Win

Tom LaBonte

Key Points

> An important initial step is selecting the right client to be the partner for your first HPI project.

> The role of a performance consultant is to help clients approach performance problems in a new way.

> Partnering with the client is the foundation for a successful HPI intervention.

> Most causes for performance gaps are found in the work environment.

> Client actions are significant enhancers and barriers of work environment change.

> A contract provides the HPI consultant and client the focus and individual accountability needed for a successful intervention.

Your background as a trainer, HR generalist, OD, or quality specialist provides a context for learning and using a systematic approach to client partnering and improved results. Selecting the right client with a performance problem that is manageable in scope, complexity, and timing is necessary for establishing a strategic partnership with value to the client, organization, and HPI department.

Here are the three major steps you need to take in selecting your first HPI project. Each of these steps is outlined in detail in the pages that follow.

1. Establish appropriate selection criteria for a client.
2. Pick a performance problem to collaborate on with a partnering client.
3. Select an intervention that you know has a good chance to succeed and write a client contract.

1. Establish Appropriate Client Selection Criteria

The criteria used by the performance consultant in selecting a client for a first intervention may make the difference between success and failure. In any organization there are many business units experiencing gaps in performance between expected results and current achievements. There are a number of managers in need of performance support. For the new performance consultant the opportunities appear overwhelming. Where do you begin?

Selecting a client to conduct an initial intervention cannot be looked upon as a transactional, one-time event. Although the goal of an initial intervention for a new performance consultant is to have a quick turnaround success, it needs to be viewed as a new beginning in establishing a longer-term client relationship. The first intervention is a new beginning in building a value proposition for the client that goes beyond single event support to providing complete performance solutions. The performance consultant needs to build a client selection profile that provides criteria for effective partnering.

What are some important selection criteria to consider as you seek the right client to be a partner in your first consulting intervention? Table 6-1 outlines some of the characteristics that may be appropriate for performance consultants to apply to client selection. It also lists the client's goals in partnering, which the performance consultant needs to understand when establishing the client relationship.

2. Pick a Performance Problem

It is not uncommon for performance consultants to work with clients who come to them with performance problems and preferred solutions all wrapped

Table 6-1. Criteria for selecting a client partner for your initial intervention.

Client Selection Criteria Used by the Performance Consultant	Performance Consultant Selection Criteria Used by the Client
• Enjoys strong leadership credibility within senior management and at all levels in organization • Has a reputation of being highly successful in achieving business goals • Demonstrates willingness to take calculated risks • Has an underperforming business unit with performance gaps appropriate for a first intervention • Demonstrates willingness to own or take responsibility for successes or misses in the business • Has decision-making authority to approve business initiatives and allocate resources • Demonstrates the willingness to invest budget, staff, facilities, and equipment in growth opportunities	• Maintains credibility within the organization as one who gets things done and can be counted on to follow a project through to successful completion • Has a reputation of being goal oriented and focused on the business • Works with clients on projects outside of the traditional scope of training • Is proactive in identifying opportunities to help the client, maintaining contact, and communicating effectively • Shares credit for successes or misses and jointly owns projects • Commits to working on an intervention and seeing it to completion • Is willing to share resources

in a neat package. Often these problems and solutions come with a timeframe that appears to the performance consultant to border on the suicidal. This scenario is closely akin to the patient who goes to the physician complaining of a stomachache, refuses to be examined, and demands the green pill as a quick cure. Physicians do not operate this way, so why should HPI practitioners commit consulting malpractice by doing what the client demands regardless of whether it is an appropriate solution?

Partnering involves establishing a relationship with the client that is long term, focused on the business and performance needs of the client, and involves providing complete solutions to the client's performance problems. For too many HPI practitioners, it is comfortable and safe to always be on the reactive end of the client relationship. Being in this mode dooms the performance consultant to existing at the whim of the client. Reactive approaches often mean being brought into projects at the last minute, cleaning up after disasters, and compromising the quality of solutions by the impossible deadlines that are imposed.

Becoming a proactive partner takes the courage and conviction to initiate meetings and discuss business needs and opportunities in a noncrisis environment. It will take time. It may take months to build a relationship of mutual understanding and trust with a potential client. But, this is the foundation that is needed to partner with a client on an intervention consulting assignment. To do so, it is beneficial to consider the perspectives (table 6-2) that the performance consultant and client have on partnering on performance problems.

Handling the Reactive Client

This reactive client relationship is too often the way of doing business in many organizations. It is true that reactive client relationships are a fact of life in most organizations. The pressing demand for speeding the product to market and heightened competitive pressures place managers in quick turnaround situations where they need performance support. In these circumstances, performance consultants streamline approaches to performance support and provide the client with the best solution that resources permit. Later the performance consultant returns to work with the client on more complete solutions to the client's performance problems. The opportunity for the performance consultant is in supporting reactive client situations while creating proactive, longer-term relationships that transcend single-event, quick-fix

Table 6-2. Intervention perspectives of the client and performance consultant.

Performance Consultant	Client
• Has new consulting competencies and tools that need to be applied	• Has an immediate business need with a short-term deadline and wants help now
• Needs a quick turnaround intervention that uses the HPI process as an early win-win	• Keeps performance solutions in mind
• Needs to create new image as a results-enhancing partner, breaking out of traditional trainer label	• Has no interest in taking the time to do assessment or measurement of results from an intervention
• Must demonstrate value to the client and organization to justify the expense of preparation and role change to performance consulting	• Does not understand performance consulting capabilities; thinks in terms of the old training department
• Thinks long term in developing strategic partnerships	• Views each project as a separate event

solutions. The performance consultant must be comfortable navigating between reactive and proactive client situations.

Your Role as Performance Consultant

Performance consultants help clients approach performance problems in a new way. The role of the performance consultant is to coach and guide the client in clearly defining the performance problem and in agreeing to use a systematic process to improving performance.

Performance consultants proactively help clients identify root causes of performance problems and the actions needed to close the gaps. Performance consultants gain the credibility needed for clients to agree to a performance intervention through effective partnering that provides the client with a new value proposition in achieving business results.

3. Select and Contract on an Intervention

How do you know which performance problem to select as a first intervention? Part of the answer is found in the preliminary assessment of performance gaps, knowledge of the client's business needs, and a realistic assessment by the performance consultant of his or her competencies, experience, and resources. Often this decision is made within days or even hours of an initial meeting with the client.

Table 6-3 is a template listing some potential causes of performance gaps and the actions that performance consultants can take to select their first performance improvement intervention. The remainder of this section is devoted to the sources of most performance gaps (work environment), barriers to change, learning and human resources barriers, as well as other important topics to consider when selecting an initial intervention project.

Barriers and Actions

Work Environment. You should expect to find that the majority of causes for performance gaps emanate from the work environment. You can also expect to find the greatest lift in performance from actions that change these work environment barriers. When selecting an intervention, consider work environment solutions before other actions. These other actions are often single-event solutions with less measurable impact over the long term than work environment changes. Because work environment barriers stem from multiple causes and require multiple solutions implemented in parallel, the

Table 6-3. Selecting a performance problem for your first intervention.

If you believe the performance gap is potentially caused by:	Then potential actions to close gaps in performance include:
Work Environment Barriers • Unusable systems, policies, procedures • Unclear position accountabilities • Inadequate staffing levels • Unreasonable workload • Ineffective workflow	**Work Environment Actions** ❑ Build common processes and models ❑ Design jobs around roles and processes ❑ Clarify scope and limits of authority ❑ Establish a performance scorecard ❑ Prioritize accountabilities ❑ Outsource where appropriate ❑ Create performance support tools ❑ Upgrade computers and software
Client Barriers • Uncommunicated or unclear goals • Lack of performance coaching • Little or no reward and recognition • Poor leadership skills and behaviors • Lack of resources to do the job	**Client Actions** ❑ Create performance management process that rewards manager coaching ❑ Establish a coaching process ❑ Develop coaching skills ❑ Provide reward and recognition tools
Learning Barriers • Poorly designed delivery methods • Fuzzy program outcomes and content • Ineffective workplace skills coaching • Ineffective measurement of value	**Learning Actions** ❑ Conduct needs assessment ❑ Provide performance based training via e-learning, computer-based training, electronic performance support systems, classroom ❑ Design workplace development tools, job aids, and templates ❑ Use knowledge management tools
Human Resources Barriers • Ineffective performance management • Poor compensation and recognition • Recruiting the right employees • High employee turnover	**Human Resources Actions** ❑ Develop employee selection profiles ❑ Develop performance criteria ❑ Redesign performance management, incentive and consequences model ❑ Implement reward/recognition program ❑ Provide challenging, meaningful work

performance consultant must carefully weigh his or her resources, competencies, and other commitments before agreeing to an intervention. It is critical to the performance consultant's success that the scope of the first intervention involves manageable work environment change.

The Client. The actions of your client are significant enhancers and barriers of work environment change. Possibly the greatest effect on employee performance in the work environment is made in helping technical managers evolve into leaders. As you select a potential intervention, look for indicators of employee stress and the leadership skills and behaviors used to build a workplace supportive of high performance.

Client resistance to change in leadership skills and behaviors can be formidable and need to be managed wisely by the new performance consultant. Identifying performance gaps with leadership barriers requires that you factor into the intervention decision the complexity, time, and expense required to develop a leadership competency model. It is used in designing and implementing executive and leadership development programs; performance management; coaching guides; recognition programs; and tools for supporting client changes in skills, behaviors, and actions.

Learning and HR. These barriers require expensive, time-consuming actions that by themselves often have little sustainable effect on performance. Selecting an intervention that is heavy on learning and HR actions may be comfortable to the performance consultant based on competencies and experience, but such an intervention often does not deliver the business results the client expects for a first intervention.

Whenever possible, choose an early intervention that is balanced between potential work environment actions, client actions, and learning and HR actions. The right intervention becomes a series of manageable actions that are limited in scope, with low to moderate complexity, and with the potential to be a quick turnaround win.

The Contract

Completing a contract with the client is the final step in selecting a client and HPI intervention. It provides the client and you with the focus and individual accountability needed for a successful intervention. The contract can be an informal memorandum or a document signed by you and the client outlining the details of the proposed intervention. The client and

Questions to Cover in Your Contract

- What is the performance gap between expected and current performance that forms the core of the proposed intervention?
- Are the proposed actions and priorities of the intervention aligned with the client's business and performance needs?
- What are the accountabilities of the performance consultant and the client?
- What are the priorities that must be addressed?
- How will success be defined?
- What resources are needed from the HPI department and the client to complete the intervention?
- What information needs to be shared? Who needs to know? How frequently will the communications occur?

performance consultant jointly develop the contract *and* agree on roles, responsibilities, goals, tasks, timelines, resources, meetings, communication, and success measures.

When It's Time to Just Say No

There will come a time when you must say no to an existing or potential client, perhaps in response to a reactive request for support, during the early steps of a proactive call on a client, or even when finalizing the contract. Saying no requires moral courage, tact, sensitivity, and the conviction that you're doing the right thing. Your decision must be based on reasonable criteria that take into account protecting the interests of the client and the organization, as well as your own best interest.

How do you know that it's time to say no to a client? You can base your decision on the five factors listed in table 6-4.

Selecting an HPI Project: A Case Study

William is a recent graduate of the performance consulting workshop. He is an experienced instructional designer and former OD specialist. He is in the process of partnering with a client in the hope of starting his first HPI intervention. William is concerned that he needs to educate potential partners

Table 6-4. When to say no to a client.

Circumstances That Dictate Saying No	What You Can Do Instead
The performance problem requires actions that are outside your competencies and experience.	Refer the client to other internal departments or an external partner for performance support.
Neither you nor the client has the resources to close the performance gap.	Contract with the client on a different intervention for which resources are available and appropriate.
There is no quantifiable performance gap.	Tell the client that carrying out an intervention without identifying a gap between expected and current performance is a waste of resources and a venture doomed to failure.
The client does not have the authority to approve an intervention and commit the resources necessary for success.	Walk away or escalate the performance problem and partner with the true client.
The client will not develop a contract with you and balks at taking joint ownership for the intervention.	Explain that the contract is the blueprint for success and without one you (the performance consultant) may be committing consulting malpractice. Leave the door open to continue discussions when the client is ready to work on the contract.

about performance consulting, how it will benefit the client, and what will be different about his new role compared to the services he provided as an instructional designer. He knows that he will need to demonstrate this new value proposition in his first intervention. This intervention must be a success that allows him to begin building a reputation for results that will lead to additional consulting business.

Mary and Jorge are two senior line managers who are at the top of William's list as potential clients. Mary is the senior vice president of sales and has a reputation as a no-nonsense, results-oriented manager. Her division is responsible for approximately 30 percent of the gross revenue of the organization. The CEO is relying on Mary's division to reach stretch targets on sales and profitability by the year's end.

In an initial meeting with Mary, William explains his role as a performance consultant and the value that the HPI process, tools, and competencies bring to potential clients. He asks her about her goals for the year, her concerns about performance, and issues that she and her division are facing. Mary confides that her biggest concern is her ability to hit stretch targets when her division is facing annual turnover rates of approximately 40 percent. This revolving door is hampering her ability to meet production goals and is consuming expensive resources in recruiting and training. She anticipates that the lost sales opportunity costs are staggering.

Mary is willing to work with William in figuring out why turnover is occurring at such high rates. She will devote resources in people and budget to solve this problem by the end of the next quarter. Mary wants to begin working with William immediately. What can he do for her and how quickly can he get to it?

William is pleased by Mary's willingness to partner, her desire to address a critical performance problem, and her willingness to commit resources and focus on resolving the turnover issue. A warning bell goes off in his mind. In the performance consulting workshop he remembers a discussion on how to do a preliminary assessment of performance problems and be sure that the scope, complexity, and competencies needed to implement a first intervention are aligned. He is also concerned about Mary's timeline. He knows enough about performance consulting and employee turnover to be cautious about overcommitting to a potential intervention before doing some homework.

William needs to discuss Mary's business issue with other members of the HPI department and do some benchmarking and a review of the literature on turnover. He promises to get back to her, and they arrange a meeting for the following week.

Jorge is the executive vice president of operations. In an initial consulting meeting, Jorge discusses his business needs and potential performance gaps with William. Jorge is very concerned about declining morale within a major department of his division. In the employee satisfaction survey conducted last quarter, the information system (IS) department had the lowest score on employee satisfaction in the organization. The data from the survey suggests that employees were tolerating some of the usual causes of dissatisfaction: pay, benefits, leadership, and communication. The main driver of dissatisfaction appears to be related to workload.

The organization had gone through several mergers in the past year and implemented a new sales and service system, all without additions to the IS staff. Jorge and his IS manager had observed some indicators of dissatisfaction in the workplace but were shocked by the results on the survey.

The CEO expects the operations division to support the implementation of several new products that are expected to generate increased sales and profitability. The IS department plays a key role in supporting line sales and service goals. Jorge asks William for suggestions on how they should address morale issues with limited resources and pressing business demands. William feels good about his initial meeting with Jorge, the rapport they are developing, and Jorge's willingness to take responsibility for solving the problem. The meeting ends with William committing to doing some preliminary analysis and returning in a week to follow up with Jorge.

William has a serious dilemma. He has identified two potential clients with serious performance problems who want help immediately. He goes over the client selection checklists and job aids (tables 6-1, 6-2, 6-3) provided at the performance consulting workshop and reviews criteria for intervention selection. He conducts a preliminary assessment of both performance problems to see which is the better intervention for his first HPI project. William recognizes that he can only support one intervention and needs to hand off one of the potential clients to another performance consultant.

Jorge and his workload performance problem appear to William to be the best fit for his competencies, experience, resources, and timeline. The turnover problem in Mary's division is a long-term intervention that is highly complex, requires the support of HR, the HPI department, operations, and some of Mary's key managers. Mary's timeline is much more aggressive than one performance consultant can influence. William recognizes that he simply doesn't have the project management and consulting expertise to lead this type of intervention as a new performance consultant. He needs an intervention of smaller scope with a better fit to his consulting skills and experience.

The HPI leader and William decide that for William's ongoing development, he needs to work on an independent intervention of manageable scope. They agree that his background in instructional systems design (ISD) and OD are more appropriate for supporting Jorge's potential intervention.

Jorge and William meet the next day to begin developing the contract for the workload intervention. William's preliminary cause analysis indicates that employee satisfaction and productivity are suffering because there are too few employees during times of peak client demand. This shortage leads to unrealistic performance expectations, a focus on quantity instead of quality of results, and high levels of employee stress.

William believes a job analysis is probably needed along with a staffing model review. Jorge agrees that this may lead to adjustment of workload, the removal of low-value tasks, and streamlined workflows needed to change the work environment. They list these activities in the contract as tasks, specifying assignments, timelines, and standards. William believes that with the available resources in operations, his relevant experience, and with the leadership of Jorge and his managers that they can begin seeing positive results in equalizing workload and reducing employee stress in about three months. They finalize the contract and begin planning the first meeting of the intervention team.

Your HPI Challenge

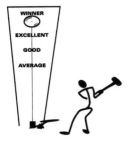

In this chapter you learned tips and techniques on how to approach selecting the right client and the right first intervention as a new performance consultant. Selecting a client with the right performance problem for a first intervention requires persistence, a systematic approach, and a focus on business improvement opportunities that the performance consultant can positively impact. The following points are recommended for your consideration as a new performance consultant starting to work on your first intervention:

✓ Partner with a client who has performance problems that are manageable, of short duration, and within your competencies and capabilities to address.

✓ Ensure that your client is willing to jointly own the intervention with you and commit the resources to successfully complete the intervention.

✓ Anticipate and firmly deal with your client's resistance during contract negotiations on the time and expense of conducting an intervention. This posture requires tact, persistence, and the willingness to provide your client with continuous education and communication.

✓ Try to underpromise and overdeliver as you negotiate outcomes and manage client expectations for the potential intervention.

✓ Build upon the success of your first intervention and market this success to generate opportunities for more performance consulting business.

✓ Capture lessons learned in this first intervention and use them as part of your continuous learning approach to being a performance consultant.

Additional Resources

Block, P. (2000). *Flawless Consulting: A Guide to Getting Your Expertise Used* (2d edition). San Francisco: Jossey-Bass/Pfeiffer.

Chang, R.Y., and M.W. Morgan. (2000). *Performance Scorecards: Measuring the Right Things in the Real World.* San Francisco: Jossey-Bass.

Fuller, J., and B. Sugrue, editors. (1999). *Performance Interventions: Selecting, Implementing, and Evaluating the Results.* Alexandria, VA: ASTD.

Kaplan, R.S., and D.P. Norton. (1996). *The Balanced Scorecard: Translating Strategy Into Action.* Boston: Harvard Business School Press.

LaBonte, T.J. (2001). *Building a New Performance Vision: Break Down Organizational Silos and Create a Unified Approach to Human Performance Improvement.* Alexandria, VA: ASTD.

Robinson, D.G., and J.C. Robinson, editors. (1998). *Moving From Training to Performance: A Practical Guidebook.* Alexandria, VA: ASTD.

Robinson, D.G., and J.C. Robinson. (1995). *Performance Consulting: Moving Beyond Training.* San Francisco: Berrett-Koehler Publishers.

Stolovich, H.D., and E.J. Keeps. (1999). *Handbook of Human Performance Technology* (2d edition). Washington, D.C.: International Society for Performance Improvement.

About the Author

Tom LaBonte is the managing director of Workplace Performance, specializing in improving performance through an integrated process to learning and workplace actions for breakthrough results. LaBonte is an HPI professional with more than 25 years' experience as a training director and HR executive in business, government, and academia. He has previously held the positions of HR executive with Centura Banks and senior vice president of performance improvement and training at PNC Bank. He has recently written a book published by the ASTD Press, *Building a New Performance Vision,* and has written numerous chapters in books and articles on performance improvement and e-learning. LaBonte served on the ASTD board and currently serves as chair of the ASTD Global Nominating Committee. He may be reached at tjlabonte@earthlink.net.

Motivational Interventions: Salary, Bonus, or That Corner Office

Sivasailam "Thiagi" Thiagarajan

Key Points

➤ Motivational interventions improve human performance by increasing the amount of commitment and persistence of performers.

➤ There are both monetary and nonmonetary motivational interventions.

➤ Performance = Ability × Environment × Motivation.

➤ Understanding different types of motivation helps you select, design, and implement the best type of motivation to achieve different goals.

➤ Both motivators and demotivators need to be considered.

➤ Interventions should be designed and implemented in accordance with organizational budget, schedule, and capacity in terms of personnel and physical resources.

➤ Select an appropriate mix of motivators.

This chapter and the two chapters that follow outline three types of interventions that you may wish to tackle as your first HPI project. Motivational interventions, the subject of this chapter, are very common and, therefore, may be applicable in your organization. Process interventions, the subject of chapter 8, require a deep organizational understanding to accomplish and are challenging to tackle. Knowledge interventions, which you will learn about in chapter 9, are key interventions and are not always, as you will learn, simply a training solution.

What Are Motivational Interventions?

Motivational interventions improve human performance by increasing the amount of commitment and persistence of performers. Monetary interventions include salary, merit pay, bonus, allowances, pension, profit sharing, and expense accounts. Nonmonetary motivational interventions include such factors as meaningfulness of work, sense of competence, availability of choices, feeling of progress, freedom to make mistakes, clear purpose, access to information, positive feedback, skill recognition, exciting vision, whole tasks, collaborative climate, milestones, celebrations, feedback from end users, removal of task barriers, mentoring, training, promotion, and job security.

Lack of motivation is the root cause of many performance problems. Also, all other types of HPI interventions involve a motivational component: the motivation to learn is a critical requirement for all training interventions, and the motivation to change is an important requirement for other types of interventions. The standard HPI process can be applied to the design and implementation of effective motivational interventions.

A Thought Experiment

An effective way to understand motivation is to interview people to find out why they do what they do. Answer these questions about your current behavior (reading this book).

1. Why are you reading this chapter right now? This is not a rhetorical question. Take a minute to think about the question and come up with an answer. You can even jot it down right here: _____

   _____

2. Did you answer question number 1? If yes, what made you take this task seriously? If no, what prevented you from taking this task seriously?

3. What other things could you be doing right now? Why did you choose to read this chapter instead of doing one of these other things?

4. Most people do things because that action fulfills a need. What need do you have that is fulfilled by reading this chapter?

5. How deep is this need? Will you continue reading if the telephone rings? Will you continue reading if there is a major earthquake? Will you stop reading for $20? How about for $200?

6. Have you read the chapter from the beginning without skipping anything? If you skipped some of the earlier paragraphs, why did you do that?

7. Let's assume that 2,532 copies of this book have been sold so far. Let's also assume that half of the people who purchased this book read this chapter. What could be the different reasons why people read this chapter? What could be different reasons why the other half of the people did not read this chapter?

8. Are you getting bored with these questions? If so, why?

This concludes the thought experiment. Thank you for your participation. Your responses will be addressed throughout subsequent sections of this chapter.

What Is Motivation?

Motivation means spurring someone to act in a certain way. Performance consultants define motivation as the psychological process that gives purpose and direction to people's behavior. Another way of defining motivation is to consider it as a state of mind that drives people to achieve personal and organizational goals.

A basic assumption in HPI stresses the importance of motivation. This formula identifies the three components of performance:

$$\text{Performance} = \text{Ability} \times \text{Environment} \times \text{Motivation}$$

For example, your performance—reading this chapter—indicates that you have

- *ability:* skills and knowledge required for reading
- *supportive environment:* sufficient light, comfortable temperature
- *motivation:* a desire for reading.

Lack of motivation is often the root cause (or at least the secondary cause) for most human performance problems. In a surprising number of situations, people do not perform in expected ways even if they have the ability and environmental support. In these situations, additional training or increased environmental support is unlikely to produce the desired performance. Worse yet, these interventions are likely to backfire and further demotivate the performer.

Even when training is the appropriate intervention, there is the additional challenge of motivating the performers to learn—and to apply—a new set of skills and concepts. Similarly, when other types of interventions are used, performance consultants still face the challenge of reducing people's resistance to change and motivating them adopt the new tools and techniques.

Types of Motivation: Intrinsic and Extrinsic

Understanding different types of motivation will help you select, design, and implement the best type of motivation to achieve different goals. Motivation falls into two different categories, intrinsic and extrinsic. The difference between these two types can be demonstrated with a simple example: If you are reading this chapter just for the fun of it, you are influenced by intrinsic motivation. If you are reading it because you have to make a presentation on the topic, design a motivation system for a client, or write a paper for a course you are taking, then you are influenced by extrinsic motivation.

Intrinsic Motivation

Intrinsic motivation occurs when the performance of a task becomes an end in itself. You are totally engaged in the task because you have a passion for what you are doing. Different people have different names for this highly motivated state (being "on a roll," "in the zone," or "in flow"), but it is always described in remarkably similar terms.

How to Tell if You Are Totally Engaged

- You don't want to do anything else.
- You are not required to perform this task.
- You are not performing the task just to receive some external reward.
- The performance is an end in itself.
- You have completely lost track of time
- You are totally immersed in the task.
- You don't pay attention to your feelings during the performance.
- You are happy, grateful, and wistful after the performance.
- You don't pay attention to what you are doing.
- Your performance seems to be effortless.
- You are not distracted by what is happening outside.

Extrinsic Motivation

Extrinsic motivation comes from factors outside of the task you are performing. Think back on your responses to the questions in the earlier thought experiment, especially to the first question about why you are reading this chapter. Decide for yourself if your reading performance is influenced by internal or external motivation. If you decide that your motivation is a combination of both types, then identify factors associated with each type.

Internal Versus External Motivation

Internal motivation (also known as self-motivation) comes from inside yourself; external motivation comes from the outside. It is important to note that the terms internal and intrinsic (and external and extrinsic) are not synonymous. For example, if you are reading this chapter because you are feeling guilty about not having done any professional reading since last October, you are under internal influence (because you are talking to yourself) but extrinsic motivation (because guilt is a reflection of the extrinsic cultural belief that you should keep up with the professional literature).

Performances that are induced by fantasies, daydreams, ego gratification, embarrassment, and potential effect on self-esteem are examples of internal motivation. Whenever you design a motivational intervention to improve other people's performance, you are creating, by definition, examples of external motivation.

External motivation can be categorized into monetary and nonmonetary motivators. Monetary incentives include salaries, allowances, in-kind salary supplement, bonuses, commissions, and benefits. Nonmonetary incentives include the desirable working conditions listed in table 7-1.

Motivators and Demotivators

Basically, two approaches enable performance consultants to develop effective motivation systems:

- adding and highlighting motivators that reinforce appropriate performance
- removing and reducing demotivators that punish appropriate performance.

Depending exclusively on the first approach will not provide an effective motivation system. Unless you systematically identify various demotivators

Table 7-1. Working conditions that exemplify nonmonetary incentives.

Category	Examples
Physical resources	Corner office Convenient parking Latest hardware and software
Personnel resources	Support staff Enlightened management Dedicated team members
Career opportunities	Career ladder Job rotation Rapid promotion
Recognition	Lunch with the chief executive officer Note of praise from a customer News item in company newsletter
Fun place to work	Playfulness Spontaneity Celebration of diversity

that hamper desirable performances, the whole purpose of the motivational system is defeated. What makes the second approach more challenging is the fact that most demotivators are hidden under a set of "undiscussables" in any organization. For example, if individuals are not rewarded because it is considered contrary to team spirit, then the demotivating impact of ignoring individual excellence will reduce everyone's performance to the lowest common denominator. Table 7-2 provides lists of motivators and demotivators typically found in most organizations.

Table 7-2. Lists of motivators and demotivators.

Motivators

access to customers	freedom to make mistakes	patents
access to information	full involvement	pay for performance
appreciation	fun	pension plan
athletic leagues	healthy competition	performance appraisal
authority	help with personal problems	personal growth
automobile	ideal geographic location	positive feedback
awards	immediate feedback	power
balanced workload	increasing competence	professional conferences
career counseling	informal atmosphere	professional friendships
career ladder	inspiring leadership	professional growth
celebrations	intellectual challenge	progress
challenging work	interesting work	promotion
choice of assignments	investment trust	recognition
clear purpose	job security	relevant tasks
club membership	leadership	royalties
collaboration	loans	sabbatical
collegiality	maternity leave	sense of choice
compatible values	meaningful work	social interaction
competitive pay	medical insurance	staff support
constructive feedback	membership in professional organizations	status
empowerment	mentoring	stimulating environment
encouragement	merit pay	stock option
entertainment allowance	networking	teamwork
entrepreneurial support	on-the-job training	telecommuting
exciting vision		tenure

(continued next page)

Table 7-2. Lists of motivators and demotivators. *(continued)*

Motivators

family allowance	opportunities for achievement	timely feedback
flexible schedule		tools and equipment
flow experiences	overtime pay	training allowance
free housing	paid vacation	travel allowance
free meals	parking	trust
freedom to innovate	participatory decision making	variety

Demotivators

avoidance of risk	insecurity	red tape
being taken for granted	irrelevant tasks	repetitive tasks
boring assignments	lack of choices	rigid schedule
bureaucracy	lack of feedback	rote activities
cynicism	lack of fringe benefits	sense of incompetence
confusing goals	lack of leadership	slow decision making
dead-end job	lack of opportunities for advancement	tolerance of poor performance
delays		
discouragement	lack of pension plan	trivial tasks
discrimination	lack of progress	unclear expectations
distrust among workers	lack of staff support	underutilization of skills
drab facilities	lack of vision	undesirable location
excessive paperwork	meaningless work	unfair treatment
excessive workload	minimal pay	unhealthy competition
frequent criticism	obstacles to performance	unnecessary rules
hierarchical structure	paranoia	unproductive meetings
hostile work environment	politics	withholding of information
hostility		

Variations in Purpose: The Three *R*s

Motivational systems can be classified according to specific purposes they emphasize. Based on this criterion, here are the three *R*s of motivational systems:

- Recruitment systems encourage competent people to work for the organization (for example, by offering a joining bonus).

- Retention systems discourage competent people from leaving the organization (for example, by giving employees annual pay increases).
- Results systems encourage competent people to accomplish more for the organization (for example, by implementing a pay-for-performance system).

Making a Decision Based on Needs

The preceding discussion of different types of motivation systems should enable you to make informed decisions about which types to include in developing the most appropriate combination for your specific needs. The design and implementation of all types of motivation systems can be accomplished through the use of a modified form of the HPI model. The next section of this chapter explores this process.

How to Design and Implement a Motivation System

Every organization has a budget, a schedule, and a limited capacity in terms of personnel and physical resources. Designing motivational interventions presents challenges concerning the efficient allocation of these limited resources.

For example, if you are planning to pay higher salaries to increase the motivational levels of employees, then something else has to be sacrificed. You may have to fire some employees to afford salary increases for the others. Then you have to increase the productivity of the remaining employees (through tools, job aids, and training) to compensate for the absence of the downsized employees. Because of this type of interdependence among performance and motivation elements, piecemeal efforts are likely to fail.

To prevent potential problems with motivation systems, it is important to adopt a systematic and systemic view. Table 7-3 outlines a procedural approach for developing a comprehensive system of motivational interventions.

Although table 7-3 implies a linear, step-by-step approach, you can use it in a flexible fashion to maximize its usefulness. Guidelines for each of the dozen steps in the checklist are briefly discussed in the sections that follow.

Analysis Activities

1. *Analyze motivational characteristics and preferences of the target population.* Organize employees at different types and levels. Interview representative

Table 7-3. Activities for developing a motivational system.

Analysis Activities

1. Analyze motivational characteristics and preferences of the target population.
2. Analyze motivators and demotivators that influence current job performance.
3. Conduct a job/task analysis.
4. Specify performance goals and related rewards.

Design Activities

5. Select an appropriate mix of motivators.
6. Design a prototype motivation system.
7. Review the system for undesirable effects.
8. Revise the motivation system.

Implementation Activities

9. Keep employees involved and informed.
10. Orient the employees to the new motivation system.
11. Modify the system based on immediate feedback.
12. Continuously monitor and upgrade the system.

members of each group to identify the types of motivators (incentives and rewards) they would like to receive and the type of demotivators (disincentives and punishers) that they would like to avoid. Through surveys and interviews, identify subgroup differences (for example between men and women, between professional and support staff, and among people with different ethnic backgrounds) and individual differences. Summarize the data in the form of matrix of different groups and preferred motivators.

2. *Analyze motivators and demotivators that influence current job performance.* Identify and analyze various motivators and demotivators that are prevalent in the organization. Review organizational policies, regulations, and standard procedures related to the use of different incentives. Prepare a balance sheet of motivators and demotivators for each job. Use the lists in table 7-2, but probe employees during interviews for additional hidden motivators and demotivators.

3. *Conduct a job/task analysis.* Identify various jobs, functions, tasks, and accomplishments. Through observation and interviews, prepare a list of routine and unusual activities on the job. Collect data on inputs, processes, and outputs associated with each job. Also, identify interactions among different jobs.

4. *Specify performance goals and related rewards.* Conclude the analyses by combining the data to prepare a list of performance goals for different groups of employees, preferred motivators and demotivators, and actual motivators and demotivators. Specify the strategic goals for the entire organization and its various functions.

Design Activities

5. *Select an appropriate mix of motivators.* Prepare a list of motivators for each group of employees. Begin by redefining base salary levels for each group. Determine the split between salary and other performance-based monetary incentives. Work out formulas for profit sharing. Identify nonmonetary incentives of different groups of employees.

6. *Design a prototype motivation system.* Construct valid, reliable, and objective measures for measuring accomplishments of people in each group. Specify the minimum amount of each type of motivator for each group. Work out a menu of additional rewards for outstanding performance. Specify how employees can personalize the motivation system to suit individual preferences. Prepare a plan for removing all current demotivators in the organization.

7. *Review the system for undesirable effects.* During this critical step, work with representative employees from different groups to check the *ABCs* of the proposed motivation system (see sidebar).

8. *Revise the motivation system.* Based on feedback from experts and representative employees, modify the motivation system to provide more adequate, balanced, and consistent rewards.

Implementation Activities

9. *Keep employees involved and informed.* Effective implementation of the motivation system begins at the first step of this systematic procedure. Throughout the developmental activity, all employees should be

Evaluate Your Motivational Intervention the ABC Way

- *A* is for adequacy: Does the motivation system provide an adequate level of rewards associated with the job performance required of the group? Are the rewards adequate when compared to alternative opportunities available to the performer?
- *B* is for balance: Does the motivation system feature horizontal balance by providing equal rewards for equal levels of performance? Does the system feature vertical balance by providing differentiated rewards for unequal levels of performance?
- *C* is for consistency: Does the motivation system directly reward the achievement of organization and job goals? Is there a close fit between the rewards and job performance requirements?

informed about the *what, why, when,* and *how* of the proposed motivation system. Also, employees should be involved in the process by providing inputs and feedback.

10. *Orient the employees to the new motivation system.* As a key step in implementing the new system, all employees should be provided an orientation to its features through brochures, announcements, and meetings.

11. *Modify the system based on immediate feedback.* The initial couple of months under the new motivation system should be treated as a pilot test. Despite careful and systematic planning, the ultimate proof of effectiveness of the motivation system is employee acceptance. During this initial stage of implementation, encourage employees to complain and to make suggestions. Based on these, the motivation system should be appropriately modified to improve its effectiveness.

12. *Continuously monitor and upgrade the system.* There is no such thing as the final version of the motivation system. The new motivation system should be perceived as a dynamic package that constantly adapts itself to changing conditions. A representative group of employees should con-

tinuously monitor changes in the industry, market conditions, and workforce characteristics to make periodic adjustments to the system.

A Case Study

The following case study is based on facts related to a motivational intervention carried out at a real organization. (Its name has been changed to protect client confidentiality.) It is not a success story, nor is it a report of a failure. Rather, it's a snapshot of what is happening with a motivation system.

SoftSkills Learning Company is a software training organization that has been in business for the past 15 years. It currently has about 50 employees divided into four divisions: instructional design, training delivery, sales, and support. Five years ago, the founder of SoftSkills decided to implement a modified form of a gainsharing motivation system that he had read about in a business journal.

Here's how the system operates: Each division head meets with a team of three employees from the division at the beginning of each financial year to come up with five goals. The goals for the division may change from one year to the next, depending on market conditions. The departmental team also comes up with appropriate metrics to measure the achievement of each goal. These measures are specified at three levels: minimum, medium, and exceptional. At the end of each year, if the division achieves its goals, its employees receive a bonus that equals a specific percent of their annual salary: Achievement of the goals at the minimum level is rewarded by a 3 percent bonus, the medium level by a 5 percent bonus, and the exceptional level by a 10 percent bonus. All employees in a division receive the same percentage irrespective of their individual contribution to the total effort.

Throughout the year, members of gainsharing teams from different departments make presentations during monthly staff meetings. These presentations deal with the mechanical and logistic details of the gainsharing system. All employees from all divisions attend the meetings in which gainsharing team members exhort participants to support enthusiastically the divisional goals and contribute their achievement goals at the exceptional level. Usual comments and questions from participants revolve around variations of "What's in it for me?"

Your HPI Challenge

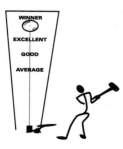

✔ As a posttest of your mastery of principles and procedures explored in this chapter, analyze the case study and identify the strengths and weaknesses of SoftSkills Learning Company's gainsharing plan as a motivation system. If the client organization were to hire you as a performance consultant, what immediate recommendations do you have for improving this motivation system?

_____

_____

_____

_____

_____

_____

_____

_____

✔ Here's a final thought experiment: What do you plan to do with the new skills and concepts that you have mastered from this chapter? What motivators and demotivators are likely to influence these application plans?

_____

_____

_____

_____

_____

_____

_____

Additional Resources

Blanchard, K.H. (1997). *Gung Ho! Turn on the People in any Organization.* New York: William Morrow.

Buckingham, M., and D.O. Clifton. (2001). *Now Discover Your Strengths.* New York: The Free Press.

Csikszentmihalyi, M. (1997). *Finding Flow: The Psychology of Engagement with Everyday Life.* New York: Basic Books.

Deci, E., and R. Flaste. (1996). *Why We Do What We Do.* New York: Penguin.

Fletcher, J.L. (1993). *Pattern of High Performance: Discovering the Way People Work Best.* San Francisco: Berrett-Koehler.

Gallwey, W.T. (2000). *The Inner Game of Work.* New York: Random House.

Lundin, S.C., H. Paul, and J. Christensen. (2000). *FISH! A Remarkable Way to Boost Morale and Improve Results.* New York: Hyperion.

Reiss, S. (2000). *Who Am I? The 16 Basic Desires That Motivate Our Actions and Define Our Personalities.* New York: Jeremey P. Tarcher/Putnam.

Spitzer, D.R. (1995). *SuperMotivation: A Blueprint for Energizing Your Organization From Top to Bottom.* New York: Amacom.

Thomas, K.W. (2000). *Intrinsic Motivation at Work: Building Energy and Commitment.* San Francisco: Berrett-Koehler.

Wlodkowski, R.J. (1999). *Enhancing Adult Motivation to Learn: A Comprehensive Guide for Teaching All Adults.* San Francisco: Jossey-Bass.

Yerkes, L. (2001). *Fun Works: Creating Places Where People Love to Work.* San Francisco: Berrett-Koehler.

About the Author

Sivasailam "Thiagi" Thiagarajan is the president of Workshops by Thiagi, an organization with the mission of helping people improve their performance effectively and enjoyably. He is also the CEO of San Francisco-based Qube, a company that provides HPI services. His long-term clients include AT&T, Bank of Montreal, Cadence Design Systems, Chevron, IBM, Intel, Intelsat, United Airlines, and Liberty Mutual. On a short-term basis, Thiagi has worked with more than 50 different organizations in high-technology, financial services, and management consulting areas. For these clients, Thiagi has consulted and conducted training in such areas as rightsizing, diversity, creativity, teamwork, customer satisfaction, HPI, and organizational learning.

Thiagi has published 40 books, 120 games and simulations, and more than 200 articles. He wrote the definitive chapters on simulations and games for *The ASTD Training and Development Handbook: A Guide to Human Resource Development* (1996) and the *Handbook of Human Performance Technology* (Jossey-Bass, 1999). He currently writes a monthly newsletter, *Thiagi GameLetter* and edits the simulation/game section in Sage Publication's journal, *Simulation & Gaming*.

Internationally recognized as an expert in multinational collaboration and active learning in organizations, Thiagi has lived in three different countries and has consulted in 21 others. For more information, point your Web browser to www.thiagi.com.

Designing and Developing Structure/Process Interventions

Roger E. Main

Key Points

➤ The HPI practitioner should always start by conducting a gap analysis to determine the current level of organizational performance compared against the desired level of performance.

➤ Examples of organizational systems include management systems, HR systems, financial systems, political systems, and social systems.

➤ Process-level interventions can have the most immediate effect on the performance of an organization or job performer.

➤ Four basic components—inputs, process controls, outputs, and resources—comprise a process.

➤ A good job performer when pitted against a bad system or process will fail every time.

Organization/Structural Interventions

Organizational structure is possibly the most critical design component of an organization. The organizational structure establishes the operating parameters of the organization and its personnel as they conduct day-to-day activities. The chosen degree of controls, hierarchy model, and standardization of processes together determine the overall effectiveness and efficiency of an organization.

You, as an HPI practitioner should always start by conducting a gap analysis to determine the current level of organizational performance compared against the desired level of performance (see chapter 4). In general, HPI practitioners do not spend enough time conducting analysis activities. Many estimate that between 40 to 50 percent of project time should be devoted to diagnostic analyses. A significant focus of this analysis work should involve assessing the overall organizational culture, politics, and business goals. A solid baseline of current performance levels should be developed at this time. By working with senior-level leadership, you can develop a clear understanding of the preferred organizational model.

Organization-level interventions include

- work redesign
- reengineering
- change management
- system engineering
- job design or redesign
- OD activities, such as team building and participative management.

An example of such an organization-level intervention is the implementation of a business system that complies with the standards of the International Organization for Standardization (ISO). The senior leadership of an organization will decide that their organization needs to achieve registration to an ISO international quality standard. To achieve the goal of registering to an ISO standard means that multiple interventions are required; the levels of interventions required are organization, system, process, and job performer.

The ISO implementation change process begins by conducting a gap analysis against the criteria in the ISO standard. This generates a gap analysis report that is presented to the senior leadership, who can then make fact-based decisions on the overall implementation plan. Timelines, resource requirements, potential organization/structural changes, and, most important, cultural changes are discussed and interventions agreed to before the change process begins.

The same process of conducting a gap analysis should be part of any change activity at the organizational level. Be it high-performance work teams, empowerment models, reengineering, or culture change, you should always start with a gap analysis. Doing so provides the HPI practitioner with a current baseline against which to measure the intervention's impact.

Table 8-1 provides definitions of some commonly used words when discussing structure/process interventions.

System-Level Interventions

System-level interventions refer to the many systems that make up an organization. Some examples are management systems, HR systems, financial systems, political systems, and social systems.

Table 8-1. Some important terminology related to structure/process interventions.

Term	Definition
Assessment	A process of determining what is and is not happening. You conduct assessments to determine system/performance gaps.
Analysis	Determining why the performance is at the level it is. Analysis helps to determine the appropriate interventions.
Business Management System	A management system based on standards such as ISO 9000, QS 9000, TL 9000, ISO 14000, and so forth.
Gap Analysis	A process of analyzing current performance against desired performance. Can be supported by published standards, performance models, and so forth.
Intervention	Action taken to solve a problem, change behaviors, improve performance, or increase outputs/outcomes.
Organization	An entity that employs people. Reference can be made to the whole organization or specific parts of an organization.
Organizational Structure	Refers to the components of the organization and how these components fit together.
Organizational Processes	Specific behavioral processes that give life to an organization. Examples are leadership, communication, decision making, and organizational change and development.
Performance	How well people perform processes/work.
Process	An activity that produces an output. A process has inputs, controls, resources, and outputs.
System Theory	An organization is seen as one element of a number of elements that act interdependently. System theory also describes the behaviors of individuals and groups within the organization.

The most important skill that the HPI practitioner needs is systems-level thinking. You must be able to analyze each of the systems and clearly understand the systems interrelationships before you determine the applicable interventions that will enable the organization to achieve the desired results.

Using the ISO example, the management system is one of the most critical systems addressed. The current ISO standard is based on eight core principles:

1. customer-focused organization
2. leadership
3. involvement of people
4. process approach
5. system approach to management
6. continuous improvement
7. factual approach to decision making
8. mutually beneficial supplier relationships.

The ISO standard also memorializes values that the organization and the organization's management must embrace and support in a visible way. Like the organization-level intervention, the HPI practitioner needs to start with a gap analysis on a system level to determine the appropriate interventions that need to be deployed to achieve the desired results.

Systems consist of many processes. For this reason, process-level analysis and interventions are core tools that an HPI practitioner would use to modify an existing, or design a new, system. The primary difference is the defined level of outputs desired. A system has definitive outputs just as a process does; system level outputs are at a higher organizational level. An example is an automobile production system. The primary output of an automobile production system is a finished automobile. Many processes are used to produce the automobile with one process becoming the input for the next. So, if you want to affect the system, you must analyze all of the supporting processes and make strategic intervention recommendations to experience system-level change.

Process-Level Interventions

Multiple processes comprise a system. Process-level interventions can have the most immediate effect on the performance of an organization, department, or job performer. To begin a process intervention, you must conduct a process-level gap analysis. The results of the gap analysis identify the component or components of a process that need attention. Additionally, the gap analysis provides you with the critical baseline data needed to gauge the return-on-investment of the interventions applied by the HPI practitioner.

Building Blocks for a Process

To conduct a process-level gap analysis, you must first understand the basic components of a process (figure 8-1). Understanding these four basic components is critical for designing and recommending process interventions.

What Are Inputs? Process inputs are all the individual items that are required to perform the process. Materials, data, components, and information are examples of inputs. Typical inputs are consumable items, which are used up in the process.

What Are Process Controls? Process controls are the information and physical controls that have been developed for the process. Drawings, specifications, procedures, education/training, performer experience, data, competitors, and information are examples of process controls.

What Are Outputs? Process outputs can be both intended and unintended. Process outputs are defined by determining the desired result of a process.

Figure 8-1. Components of a process.

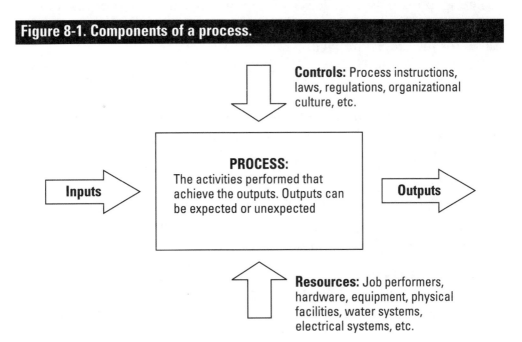

Typically, this is determined from customer requirements and or specifications. The customer can be either internal or external. Completed purchase orders, finished product, shipped product, received product, and paid employees are examples of process outputs.

What Are Resources? Process resources are the equipment, systems, and human resources required to perform the process. Heating, water, and electrical systems; physical plant; equipment and machinery; and personnel are examples of process resources. Resources are not consumed in the process. They remain available for the next run of the process.

Tinkering With Processes

You will find often that more than one process component needs to be addressed to achieve the desired process results. Each process can be an input or control for another process or processes. You can enhance your understanding of the process interrelationships in the performance system being addressed by drawing process maps that illustrate the process relationships (see chapter 3). This step enables the HPI practitioner to understand the potential effects of a process intervention on other process in the performance system. Many times it is necessary to expand the basic process model to include two additional components—suppliers on the front end of the process and customers on the back end of the process. Many times when analyzing process issues, defective supplier materials and/or unclear or undocumented customer expectations turn out to be root or contributing causes for the process problems.

Specific interventions that the HPI practitioner can apply to process improvement are the following:

- *Problem-solving or process improvement models:* These are systematic approaches that focus on a problem, identify root causes, and develop and implement solutions and action plans.
- *Flowcharts:* These are graphic tools for documenting and understanding the flow or sequence of events in a process.
- *Process control systems:* Data can be used as feedback on how a process is performing. Statistical process control is an example of a process control system.
- *Collection, organization, and reporting of data and information:* You can develop methods and systems for assembling and reporting

---

Following the "Plan, Do, Check, Act" Model

There are many standard process improvement models for making improvements. All attempt to provide a repeatable set of steps that a team or individual can learn to follow. One of the more popular models is Deming's "plan, do, check, act" (PDCA) continuous improvement model (Garbor, 1990). The steps that you would follow on the PDCA model would be as follows:

- *Plan:* Determine the process (or problem) that needs to be addressed and determine the improvement opportunity. Analyze and document the current process components. Determine and document the possible causes of the problem and get agreement on the root cause(s). Develop cost-effective and implement solutions, action plans, and, most important, targets for improvement.
- *Do:* Implement the solutions, action plans, and process changes.
- *Check:* Track, analyze, and evaluate the result of the change against the previously defined targets for improvement.
- *Act:* Based on the analysis from the previous step, reflect and act on the lessons learned.

---

information for the job performer to use to make decisions or adjust the process.

- *Gap analysis:* This process identifies missing process elements or undocumented procedures.

Job Performer Level Interventions

The final level of organizational and process level interventions is at the job performer level. The job performer works in an organization that is made up of numerous system and system processes. A fundamental rule that every HPI practitioner must understand is that a good job performer when pitted against bad systems or processes will fail every time. No matter how hard the job performer tries, the system or process overrides his or her actions every time. Only after thoroughly addressing the organizational, system, and process levels should the HPI practitioner focus on the job performer level.

Unfortunately, in today's businesses, the job performer is the primary target of improvement interventions. To address the job performer level, you must understand all the components that affect a job performer's ability to achieve the desired outcome of a process. And remember: It's the process/system, NOT the job performer!

It Takes TIME for Top Job Performance

Figure 8-2 shows a performance system diagnostic model. This model enables the HPI practitioner to analyze a performance issue by focusing on four key interrelated components. The model uses an acronym of TIME to diagnose problems with the job performer's work and work environment, and the supporting clock mechanisms correlate with the organizational structures and systems that either support or hinder job performance.

For the performance clock to run smoothly and on time, all four components must run in harmony, just as a human performance system does. Each of the four components depends on the others. Take any one away and the clock slows or stops. The loss of one of the components may not necessarily cause the clock to stop; the clock may just gradually start to lose time (figure 8-3).

Figure 8-2. The TIME performance clock model.

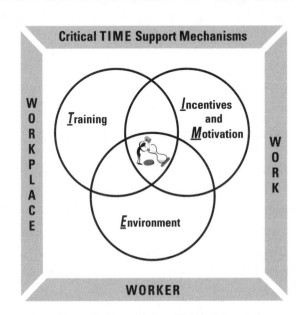

Source: Reprinted with permission of R. Main & Associates.

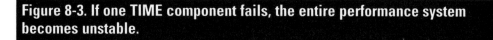

Figure 8-3. If one TIME component fails, the entire performance system becomes unstable.

The analogy of TIME can serve as a mental memory jogger to ensure that your analysis covers all parts of the performance clock.

- *Training:* The *T* in TIME. The goal of training is to provide workers with the knowledge, skills, and abilities to perform their work.

- *Incentives and motivation:* The *IM* in TIME. These are the intrinsic and extrinsic factors that affect a person's will to perform. All factors internal and external to the worker should be reviewed.

- *Environment:* The *E* in TIME. These are the extrinsic environmental factors that affect a person's work and working environment.

- *TIME support mechanisms:* The performance clock's frame. These factors represent the cultural environment and the relationship of work, worker, and workplace. They must all be aligned properly to support the performance system.

The center of the performance clock is where all of the elements merge to form the point of optimal job performance. At that point, everything is in place for a performer to perform the job at the highest level of proficiency. Every element is in perfect harmony, and the clock's framework is providing all the support necessary to keep the clock running all the time and on time.

Unfortunately, in today's business world this point of optimal performance is seldom achieved; experience indicates that organizations use less than 10 percent of a job performer's capabilities. The other 90 percent of the job performer's capabilities are utilized outside of the job environment.

The performance clock is an easy-to-understand performance system model. To remember the key components of a performance system, keep asking the following question: Do the performers have the right TIME to achieve peak performance?

How to Get Started

The following questions are sufficient for a high-level starting point for a system diagnostic:

- Do the workers have the right training?
- Are sufficient incentives to perform present?
- Do the workers have the motivation to perform?
- Is the work environment supporting them?
- Is there a shared commitment and vision that align the work, the worker, and the workplace?

Getting the answers to these five questions will help you develop a foundational picture of the current performance system and its performance level. In addition to the five questions, conducting a SWOT (strength, weakness, opportunities, and threats) analysis on the performance system can provide additional valuable analysis data. However, these models are only the beginning of an in-depth performance system analysis.

The performance clock can be an effective tool for intervention selection and grouping. Refer back to figure 8-2. There are four major components of the performance clock. Table 8-2 lists intervention groups in relation to the performance clock's components.

The Spectrum of Interventions

Designing and developing structure and process interventions are critical skills that the HPI practitioner must possess. Numerous interventions are required to be able to address each of these levels. Systems thinking and an understanding of organizational cultures and change management processes are critical to the success of the HPI practitioner. Numerous resources are avail-

Table 8-2. Performance clock intervention grouping.

Performance Clock Component	Intervention Group
Training	Interventions that support the acquisition of knowledge, skills, and abilities
Incentives and Motivation	Interventions designed to motivate the desired human performance
Environment	Interventions designed to adjust or modify the work environment
Clock Frame	Interventions designed to align the key organizational structural components of work, worker, and workplace

able for the HPI practitioner to develop these skills, including workshops, professional workshops, and books.

The intervention levels are hierarchal, beginning with the organization, then to systems, to processes, and finally ending with the job performer. If significant change is desired, the interventions must be targeted at the organization or system level. Incremental change is achieved through process- and job-performer-level interventions. Of course, the most challenging levels to work at are the top two, the organization and the system.

Your HPI Challenge

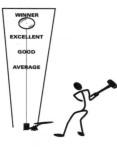

Your HPI challenge is to "think out of the box." Systems thinking and understanding have become an absolute must for the HPI practitioner. Whenever you start a new project consider the following questions.

✓ Are you focusing on systems/processes or on the job performer?

_____

_____

_____

✓ Have you completed a gap analysis and truly understand the performance issues at hand?

_____

_____

_____

✓ Have you identified more than one potential intervention? Using the TIME model, you should have identified a minimum of one intervention for each TIME element.

_____

_____

_____

_____

_____

✓ Have you fallen into the training solution trap?

_____

_____

✓ Have you developed a basic toolkit for systems and process analysis?

_____

_____

Reference

Garbor, A. (1990). *The Man Who Discovered Quality: How W. Edwards Deming Brought the Quality Revolution to America.* New York: Penguin Books.

Additional Resources

Esque, T.J., and P.A. Patterson, editors. (1998). *Getting Results: Case Studies in Performance Improvement.* Amherst, MA: HRD Press and International Society for Performance Improvement.

Gilbert, T.F. (1996). *Human Competence: Engineering Worthy Performance* (2d printing, tribute edition). Amherst, MA: HRD Press.

Hale, J. (1998). *The Performance Consultant's Handbook.* San Francisco: Pfeiffer.

Hale, J. (1998). *The Performance Consultant's Fieldbook: Tools and Techniques for Improving Organizations and People.* San Francisco: Jossey-Bass.

James-Catalano, C.N. (1996). *Researching on the World Wide Web: Spend More Time Learning, Not Searching.* Rocklin, CA: Prima Publishing.

Langdon, D. (1995). *The New Language of Work.* Amherst, MA: HRD Press.

Langdon, D.G, K.S. Whiteside, M.M. McKenna, editors. (1999). *The Intervention Resource Guide: 50 Performance Improvement Tools.* San Francisco: Jossey-Bass.

Mager, R.F., and P. Pipe. (1997). *Analyzing Performance Problems.* Atlanta: The Center for Effective Performance.

Norman, D.A. (1998). *The Invisible Computer.* Cambridge, MA: The MIT Press.

Robinson, D.G., and J.C. Robinson, editors. (1998). *Moving From Training to Performance.* San Francisco: Berrett-Koehler.

Robinson, D.G., and J.C. Robinson. (1996). *Performance Consulting: Moving Beyond Training.* San Francisco: Berrett-Koehler.

Stolovitch, H.D., and E.J. Keeps, editors. (1992). *Handbook of Human Performance Technology.* San Francisco: Jossey-Bass.

Swanson, R.A. (1996). *Analysis for Improving Performance.* San Francisco: Berrett-Koehler.

About the Author

Roger E. Main is a performance consultant and ISO management representative with the Metropolitan Community Colleges Business and Technology College in Kansas City, Missouri. In 1995, Main launched his own consulting firm (R. Main & Associates), which specializes in helping organizations improve their current systems and processes.

He has written articles, book chapters, research reports, and manuals on various aspects of instructional and performance technology. He is a frequent speaker and presenter for major companies and professional associations.

Main served as the 1998–1999 president of the award-winning Kansas City chapter of the International Society for Performance Improvement. Contact Main via email at REMain@att.net.

Knowledge Interventions: Training Is Not Always the Answer

Donald J. Ford

Key Points

➤ Training is only one of a number of knowledge interventions.

➤ To design and develop good knowledge interventions, HPI consultants need to follow a systematic process based on sound principles of instructional design.

➤ Creating knowledge interventions requires a design phase and a development phase.

➤ The design phase encompasses 12 tasks.

➤ The development phase is made up of eight tasks.

➤ A good tool for working with knowledge interventions is the ASTD Learning Technologies Classification System.

Although training immediately comes to mind when thinking of knowledge, this category of interventions includes anything that increases organizational and individual knowledge, including the following:

- information
- coaching and mentoring

- job aids
- expert and knowledge management systems
- electronic performance support systems (EPSS)
- assessment centers
- e-learning systems
- classroom training.

All knowledge interventions share common characteristics. First, they respond to performance gaps in knowledge and information. Second, they are targeted to meet specific audience needs. Third, they leverage technology where possible to provide the most efficient and effective learning experience. Finally, they rely upon a systematic approach to design and development that ensures the right content is available at the right time in the right medium.

The World of Knowledge Interventions

Once upon a time, knowledge interventions could be summed up in one simple word: training. Today, the world has become much more complex and the knowledge interventions available to HPI consultants have grown in complexity to match increased capabilities and client demands. Knowledge interventions are an appropriate response to performance gaps attributable to a lack of knowledge, skill, aptitude, attitude, or information. You know one of these causes is at the root of a performance gap when you uncover one or more of the following conditions:

- Performers are being asked to do something new or different than they have done in the past.
- Performers are unable to meet current or future performance standards because they don't know how to.
- Performers lack critical information that prevents them from meeting desired performance standards.
- Performers lack the capacity or the proper attitudes that underlie desired performance.

You will encounter some terminology when working with knowledge interventions. Review the definitions given in table 9-1 for any terms that are unfamiliar to you.

Table 9-1. A miniglossary of knowledge intervention terms.

Term	Definition
Design Blueprint/ Document	A training document that summarizes and gives examples of proposed training solutions prior to the complete development of those solutions
Distribution Method	The way that information, knowledge, or skill is delivered to the learner
E-Learning	The use of electronic technology, especially the Internet, to provide training and information to boost performers' knowledge and skills
Electronic Performance Support System (EPSS)	A system that provides information, knowledge, or skill to performers while they work using electronic technology
Intervention	Activities or tasks that are designed to improve organizational and individual performance
Job Aid	A tool that helps performers accomplish their work and that is used in real time
Learning Method	The way that individuals and groups learn new knowledge, skills, and attitudes
Presentation Method	The way that information, knowledge, or skill is formatted for the learner

Importance of Knowledge Interventions

Although many HPI experts have illustrated the perils of prescribing knowledge interventions to solve non-knowledge performance problems, no one is suggesting that knowledge interventions are about to become obsolete. In fact, the need for increased knowledge and skill is accelerating at work, driven by the relentless competition inherent in a global economy. Organizations that cease learning will stop improving themselves and eventually be driven out of business by better competitors.

The key to leveraging knowledge is to make it available whenever and wherever performers need it to help them do their jobs. Equally important is to apply knowledge solutions only when they appropriately address gaps in skills and information. Because knowledge interventions are typically costly and time consuming to build, they should be applied sparingly to address critical knowledge gaps, rather than liberally applied to all kinds of performance problems for which they are ill suited.

Important Concepts To Remember

To design and develop good knowledge interventions, HPI consultants need to follow a systematic process based on sound principles of instructional design. The instructional system design (ISD) model separates design and development into two distinct phases and sets of tasks. In the design phase, the basic concepts and structure of knowledge interventions and the project management requirements and organization come to life. In the development phase, learning materials, tests, and assessments are built, tested, and eventually moved into full-scale production. By the end of these two phases, the knowledge intervention is ready to be implemented.

Design Phase

The design phase relies on the performance and cause analyses for inputs. As figure 9-1 shows, design occurs along two simultaneous tracks: creating an instructional design and building the project management structure to oversee the rest of the knowledge design, development, implementation, and evaluation phases.

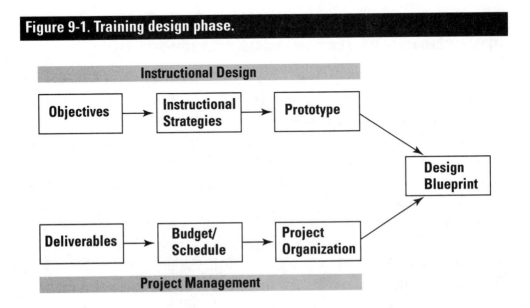

Figure 9-1. Training design phase.

Instructional Design. The instructional design phase consists of three key tasks: writing learning objectives, specifying instructional strategies, and developing a prototype.

Objectives are the logical starting point for training design because they clearly state the goals of the training. Learning objectives have four components. Two are required and two are optional:

- a statement of the target behavior, in the form of an action verb (required)
- a statement of the content or task, in the form of a noun or noun phrase (required)
- a statement of the conditions under which the learner will perform the objective (optional)
- a statement of the standard or criterion that the learner will have to meet to master the objective (optional).

The second step in the ISD process is specifying instructional strategies. These are the various processes by which training presents information and knowledge and the opportunities to practice that are afforded learners. Instructional strategies include many different processes, depending on the behaviors and content to be learned. One way to think of instructional strategies is along a continuum of active versus passive learning. On the passive end of the spectrum are strategies like lecture, reading, and question-and-answer sessions. On the active end of the spectrum are strategies like trial and error, simulations, role plays, and discussion. Generally, more active strategies produce better learning results and are preferred by adult learners.

Another way to select instructional strategies is to consider the best one to meet a particular learning objective. Objectives related to knowledge or information acquisition can be met using such strategies as lecture, video, reading, case study, and visual models. Objectives related to skill building can be met using discussion, role play, drill and practice, games, simulations, and demonstrations. Effective skill building also requires evaluative feedback to positively reinforce the things that learners are doing correctly and to constructively change the things they are doing wrong. This feedback may be oral or written, but it is most effective when given immediately after the performance in an atmosphere free of fear and negative criticism.

The third element of instructional design is prototyping. Rapid prototyping is a technique borrowed from engineering that involves creating rough drafts and small working samples of training products and programs for the purpose of early client reviews and learner input. Prototypes may consist of storyboards, templates, sample modules, and other working models. By allowing clients to review early working prototypes, the development of training can be accelerated and costly revisions can be minimized. For e-learning interventions, prototyping can save valuable time and money. The key is to prepare materials only to the point where they can be tried out and easily modified if changes are needed.

Project Management. The project management phase also consists of three primary tasks: determining the client deliverables, creating a budget and schedule, and setting up a project organization.

The first step of the project management process is to define the deliverables that the client expects to receive. A deliverable is the product of an instructional design process. In a macro sense, a training deliverable is a unit of instruction such as a module, workshop, or course. In a micro sense, deliverables typically include all the products used in training, including workbooks, manuals, lesson plans, instructor guides, overheads, audiovisual materials, videos, tests, teaching aids, reference materials, and job aids.

For most clients, defining the deliverables is a critical step, because that is the tangible thing that they are paying for. For the instructional designer, defining the deliverables is typically a matter of selecting an instructional method, a presentation method, and a delivery method from the wide range of choice available.

The second step in the project management plan is to create a schedule and a budget for the training. The schedule is a complete set of the tasks that need to be performed and an estimated amount of time to complete each task. Schedules typically include a small percentage of slack time, or time during which no activity is scheduled. If the project runs ahead of schedule, slack time can be removed, and the project can finish early. But, if the project runs behind schedule, slack time may be used to compensate for delays and still finish the project on time.

The project budget is a function of the schedule and the cost of the resources to be used on the project. Training budgets typically break costs into two components: labor and nonlabor. Labor costs include time for instructional designers, administrative support, and management. Nonlabor costs include materials, multimedia production, publishing and printing, equipment, software, travel, supplies, and overhead expenses. Budgets can be assembled with the aid of project management or spreadsheet programs, such as Microsoft Project or Excel software.

The final phase of project management involves creation of a project organization to manage the design, development, and implementation of the intervention. Activities during this phase include selecting a project sponsor and champion from the client organization, appointing a project manager (often a performance consultant), and selecting the project staff. Staff members include instructional designers, material developers, multimedia specialists, information technology specialists for learning technologies, subject matter experts, administrative support, and anyone else who can assist the project team to complete its work.

The culmination of the design phase is a design blueprint or document that describes the knowledge intervention in sufficient detail so that the client knows exactly what the finished product will look like. Analogous to an architectural blueprint, the design document translates the concept of a knowledge intervention into a concrete form that the client can review and modify if need be before the bulk of a project's resources have been committed. It should include the following elements:

- summary of the cause analysis
- learning objectives
- prerequisites (if any)
- content outline
- learning methods
- presentation/delivery methods
- practice activities
- list of training deliverables
- assessment/test specifications
- evaluation plan
- budget
- schedule.

The client should review this document and approve it before moving to the development phase.

The Development Phase

During the development phase, eight critical tasks occur, as shown in figure 9-2. The development phase is the time for you to roll up your sleeves and begin to produce training/information materials in volume. It has all the hallmarks of a production environment—large volumes of material, intensive effort by many people, tight deadlines, and, all too often, stress for everyone involved. To get through this phase unscathed, it is essential to have a good plan of attack, beginning with a clear notion about the key components of the development phase.

Draft Materials and Assessments. The first step is to draft materials and assessments using computer templates and other timesaving devices. The materials may be print-based or multimedia-based. Word processing and

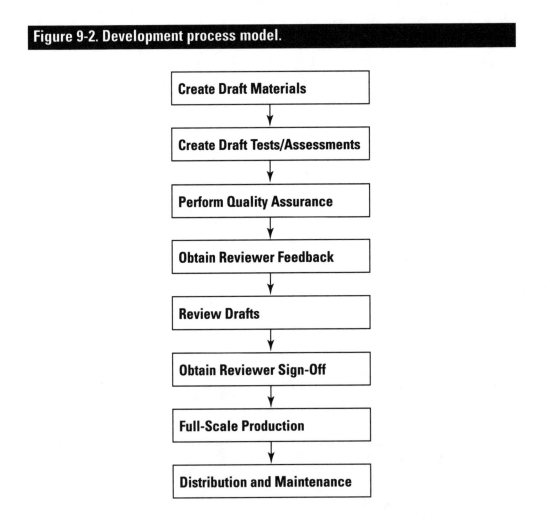

Figure 9-2. Development process model.

desktop publishing software are used to create print-based materials, often using a template that automates the formatting of text to ensure consistency. Tests and assessments should be created from a set of test specifications that describe the content domain, the learning objectives, the format of questions and answers, and the standards for correcting the test. Multimedia-based materials may include graphics, audio, video, other visuals, and the software required to display it. Often, experts in these areas who serve as subcontractors on the training development project create these materials.

Quality Assurance. The draft materials should be reviewed to determine if they meet the quality requirements of the client. The first step is an internal quality review, usually performed by the project manager or instructional designer. The internal review checks for adherence to the design blueprint and consistency across multiple modules, courses, and developers. After the internal review, the client should check the drafts for external quality, which is a reflection of the client's requirements, desires, and needs. Clients may request changes to materials to better reflect their suitability and accuracy for the intended audience. Changes that are outside the scope of the project, such as adding new content or deliverables, generally result in a negotiated revision to the budget and schedule. Those within scope are incorporated into the final draft.

Revisions and Final Approval. After all the reviews are completed, the training materials are revised and resubmitted for final client approval. A pilot test often occurs to determine how the materials will work in practice and to iron out any last-minute bugs. Before proceeding, the client should provide a formal sign-off to signal the next phase of development: full-scale production. If the client wants additional changes, another cycle of revision and approval may be required. If the client refuses to approve the final draft, the project cannot move forward until the objections have been addressed to the satisfaction of the client.

Production, Distribution, and Maintenance. After the client grants final approval, the project enters full-scale production. This is when the remainder of the development work occurs, including final publication of print materials and final production of multimedia materials.

The last step in the development process is to consider how materials are to be distributed and maintained. Distribution and maintenance issues are often negotiated as part of the training contract up front. If they are handled later, a separate agreement may be required to handle these critical issues and ensure that training programs are maintained and ready to use when needed.

Case Study: Training New Hires for a Customer Service Call Center

As an example of the complexity of choices available today, consider a hypothetical example of a request for training to support a new customer service call center that a large financial institution is planning to open in a year. The client authorizes a needs assessment, which reveals that the 200 newly hired employees who will staff the call center will need extensive training in customer service, telephone techniques, conflict resolution, problem solving, computer software, telephone system operations, product knowledge, and the company's policies and procedures.

Given the large amount of training to be conducted and the fact that it all must be designed and delivered within a year, the ISD team assigned to work on this project begins to consider the various delivery options available. First, they classify the training needs by skill type (table 9-2).

The Knowledge Intervention for Communication Skills

Next, the team considers the various delivery options suited to each of these four skill types. Because they require human interaction, communication skills

Table 9-2. Skills and training required by new hires for the customer service call center.

Skill Type	Training Needs
Communication skills	Customer service Telephone techniques Conflict resolution
Analytical skills	Problem solving
Business skills	Policies and procedures Product knowledge
Technical skills	Computer software Telephone operations

would be good candidates for classroom learning involving small groups of 10 to 20 to allow maximum interaction among learners. Instructional strategies for these skills would include role plays, case studies, videos, and overheads. Based on the instructional strategies, the designer would generate a list of deliverables, set down learning objectives, define the content for the training, and estimate the time required to learn it.

The Knowledge Intervention for Analytical Skills

Let's turn now to the next skill area—analytical problem-solving skills. Once again, problem solving is a skill involving human interaction, especially as practiced in a call center, so this skill lends itself best to classroom training. Like the communications training described above, the problem-solving course would need a similar set of materials, with extensive use of case studies and role plays of typical customer problems that call center employees will be asked to resolve.

The Knowledge Intervention for Business Skills

The business skills portion of the call center training covers industry knowledge of financial products and company knowledge of policies and procedures affecting customers. Because this kind of knowledge is contained primarily in reference manuals and books and is largely used as background information, a self-study approach to learning these skills would work well. The designers could develop a self-study workbook to guide learners through the existing product and policy materials, including exercises and quizzes to check for understanding.

An innovative approach that makes particular sense in a call center environment for delivering the policies and procedures knowledge would be the use of online reference materials through EPSS. The company's relevant customer policies and procedures could be put in digital format, loaded onto the call center's server, and made available on each employee's desktop. This might be done in a simple Windows help file, searchable by key words and topics, or via a company intranet and Web browser, where hypertext and other interactive features of the World Wide Web could be turned to good advantage. If this kind of online reference were combined with an initial self-study course on the material, then employees would be able to learn the foundation concepts without having to memorize the details, because these would be available whenever needed.

The Knowledge Intervention for Technical Skills

Finally, call center employees would need to learn a variety of technical skills, including the computer software running on the call center's PCs and the use of the center's interactive voice recognition telephone system. These technical skills would lend themselves ideally to computer-based training (CBT) or Web-based training (WBT), because learners would be using PCs to learn these skills anyway.

A well-designed tutorial could be built into the call center's database software so that employees could learn at their desks at their own pace. For practice, a special training database, replicating the company's real customer database, could be provided to employees, who would then be able to simulate their work environment almost exactly. For employees who lack any PC skill, a brief classroom orientation should be enough to teach them some basic computer literacy. At that point, they would be ready to use the CBT at their desks.

Although the telephone systems could also be easily taught through CBT, the company might decide that what employees need to know to operate their telephones could be learned on the job. To ensure that this learning occurs in an efficient and effective manner, the instructional design team could create a structured on-the-job training course that supervisors or senior-level employees could easily deliver to small groups of employees or even one-on-one. The course would include a lesson plan, props, visuals, learner job aids, and a learning evaluation.

Case Study Results

You've seen in this example how a single training project, involving the creation of a new call center, could productively use a variety of delivery mechanisms and generate an equally diverse set of deliverables. The instructional designers on this project would be responsible for the following deliverables:

- two participant workbooks
- two instructor's guides
- role plays
- two case studies on customer service and problem solving
- a video on conflict resolution

- a video on problem solving
- color overheads
- two written quizzes
- a self-study workbook
- a CBT or WBT program
- an online reference program (EPSS)
- a structured on-the-job training course.

Job Aid: Knowledge Intervention Selection

One of the best tools for knowledge interventions is the ASTD Learning Technologies Classification System (Piskurich & Sanders, 1998). Based on the combination of three separate methods that all knowledge interventions contain, it is a comprehensive way to look at the world of knowledge interventions and specify the right amount of technology. The three methods embedded in any knowledge intervention are

- *learning method:* the way that performers will learn new knowledge and information
- *presentation method:* the way that knowledge and information are formatted for performers
- *distribution method:* the way that knowledge and information are delivered to performers.

As table 9-3 illustrates, the Learning Technologies Classification System enables you to select a method from each column and assemble a knowledge intervention that meets a client's unique needs.

As an example of how to use the classification system, take another look at the case study. The choices of deliverables were based on a careful consideration of the three methods listed above and the best options among them to meet the client's needs. Table 9-4 shows how several of the deliverables were assembled using the classification system.

It is possible to assemble a variety of other viable options to address the same learning content. Of course, not all options are viable. For example, a role play presented via one-way video over cable TV, or a group discussion presented with electronic text distributed by audiotape is not a viable option because some components are mutually exclusive or illogical.

Table 9-3. Training classification system.

Learning Methods	Presentation Methods	Distribution Methods
❏ Action Learning	❏ 3-D Modeling	❏ Audiotape
❏ Apprenticeship	❏ Art/Illustration	❏ Cable TV
❏ Case Study	❏ Audio	❏ CD-I (Interactive)
❏ Demonstration	❏ Classroom Trainer	❏ CD-ROM
❏ Discussion	❏ Computer (CBT)	❏ DVD (Digital Video Disk)
❏ Drill and Practice	❏ Dialogue	❏ Electronic Mail
❏ Expert Panel	❏ E-Mail	❏ Floppy Disk
❏ Game	❏ EPSS	❏ Internet
❏ Homework	❏ Groupware	❏ Intranet
❏ Lecture	❏ Interactive TV	❏ Local Area Network/ Wide Area Network
❏ Mentoring	❏ Internet (IBT)	❏ Laserdisc
❏ On-the-Job Training	❏ Job Aid	❏ Live Speech
❏ Project	❏ Learning Group	❏ Mail
❏ Role Play	❏ Multimedia	❏ Satellite TV
❏ Self-Study	❏ Print	❏ Simulator/Tactile Gear
❏ Simulation	❏ Videoconference	❏ Telephone
❏ Small Group Activity	❏ Television	
❏ Trial and Error	❏ Video	
	❏ Virtual Reality	

SOURCE: Piskurich, G., and E. Sanders. (1998). *ASTD Models for Learning Technologies.* Alexandria, VA: ASTD.

Table 9-4. Examples based on the Learning Technologies Classification System.

Topic	Learning Method	Presentation Method	Distribution Method
Customer service	Role play	Classroom trainer	Live speech
Business policies and procedures	Reading	EPSS	Intranet
Computer software	Programmed instruction	CBT	LAN (local area network)

SOURCE: Piskurich, G., and E. Sanders. (1998). *ASTD Models for Learning Technologies.* Alexandria, VA: ASTD.

Using Knowledge Interventions

This chapter has presented basic guidelines for designing and developing knowledge interventions that address gaps in performers' information, knowledge, or skill. The world of knowledge interventions is growing rapidly, due to the growth of electronic technologies and the complexity of organizational problems. To design and develop effective knowledge interventions, you should follow a systematic process of designing and developing interventions using sound principles of instructional design, project management, and performance consulting. Job aids, such as the Learning Technologies Classification System, can assist you in choosing the right interventions to match the unique needs of clients and performers.

Your HPI Challenge

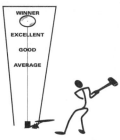

Table 9-5 presents a series of exercises to help you apply your new learning about knowledge interventions.

Table 9-5. Thinking about the best ways to use knowledge interventions.

1. Tie to business results.

You've been asked to provide training support to a new software program launch that will enable sales order entry via a company Website. You've also been asked to help the project leader calculate a benefit-cost ratio for the project and to help the executive committee prioritize this project in this year's budget review.	✓ How would you go about determining the value of this project to the organization? _____ _____ ✓ What steps would you take to identify the potential costs and benefits of this program? _____ _____ ✓ How could you isolate the effectiveness of the training portion? _____ _____

(continued next page)

Table 9-5. Thinking about the best ways to use knowledge interventions. *(continued)*

2. Use training only to solve knowledge problems.

You receive a request from a manager to retrain a group of employees on time management, when you know the problem is a poorly designed work process.

✓ How would you address this problem with the manager and get her to consider other possible root causes?

_____

_____

_____

_____

_____

3. Streamline when necessary and be creative.

You are assigned to lead a project that includes a new public relations customer service program and training for employees to back it up. You're on a very tight deadline and working with inadequate resources.

✓ Which essential design and delivery elements would you insist on following and which could be downplayed?

_____

_____

_____

_____

_____

Reference

Piskurich, G., and E. Sanders. (1998). *ASTD Models for Learning Technologies.* Alexandria, VA: ASTD.

Additional Resources

ASTD Website. www.astd.org.

Dick, W., and L. Carey. (1990). *The Systematic Design of Instruction* (3d edition). New York: HarperCollins.

Electronic Performance Support System Website. www.epss.com.

Ford, D. (1999). *Bottom-Line Training.* Woburn, MA: Butterworth Heinemann.

Gery, G. (1991). *Electronic Performance Support Systems.* Boston: Weingarten.

International Society for Performance Improvement Website. www.ispi.org.

Rothwell, W., and H.C. Kazanas. (1998). *Mastering the Instructional Design Process.* San Francisco: Jossey-Bass.

Stolovitch, H.D., and E.J. Keeps, editors. (1992). *Handbook of Human Performance Technology.* San Francisco: Jossey-Bass.

Web-Based Training Information Center. www.filename.com/wbt/index.html.

About the Author

Donald J. Ford is a training and performance improvement consultant specializing in instructional design and process improvement. He has worked in the field of HRD for 20 years, including training management positions at Southern California Gas Company, Magnavox, Allied-Signal, and Texas Instruments.

Ford has published 35 articles and three books on topics in training, education, and management including *Bottom-Line Training: How to Design and Implement Training Programs That Boost Profits.* He has presented at the annual conferences of ASTD and the International Society for Performance, ASTD quality symposia, Academy of Management, International Quality and Productivity Conference, and American Educational Research Association.

The Research Is In: Stakeholder Involvement Is Critical

Mary Broad

Key Points

➤ Most investments in training to improve performance are lost because new knowledge and skills are not transferred to the workplace. The achievement of any desired change requires the commitment of HPI practitioners, managers, and other stakeholders.

➤ HPI practitioners must identify and involve key stakeholders in important system components, throughout the entire change process.

➤ Managers must give learners prior information about the need to transfer new knowledge and skills, and provide significant additional support to the change effort.

➤ Other stakeholders must determine what actions they can take (before, during, and after any intervention) to support one or more of the six essential factors that sustain performance.

➤ Stakeholders are the best communicators to their peers and other stakeholder groups.

Key stakeholders must be actively involved in any performance improvement effort to ensure accomplishment of the desired results. As an HPI professional, you must take the initiative to organize this stakeholder involvement. Without it, barriers and difficulties in the workplace interfere with full performance by employees and block the desired organizational results. Here are some important attributes of your HPI role:

- recognizing current and potential performance problems
- educating managers and other employees about essential factors to support performance
- identifying key stakeholders in performance and results
- involving stakeholders in every step of the HPI process
- helping stakeholders identify specific strategies by which they can support learning and performance
- getting stakeholder agreement on evaluation criteria that will measure success.

Companies Want—But Don't Always Get—a High-Performing Workforce

Most contemporary organizations have significant problems obtaining the desired workforce performance. A Conference Board study found that 98 percent of responding U.S. and European organizations had problems in getting the performance they wanted from the workforce (Csoka, 1994).

Many HPI professionals recognize that most investments in training to improve performance are lost because new knowledge and skills are not transferred to the workplace. "Typically, less than 30 percent of what people learn is ever actually used on the job" (Robinson & Robinson, 1998).

This pervasive lack of performance is caused by the weakness or absence of one or more major factors in the work environment, all of which must be provided by stakeholders to support full performance. These factors and the key stakeholders with most leverage in providing them are shown in table 10-1.

Human performance improvement is a systemic process that seeks to identify and resolve root problems, not just surface symptoms. It also considers all

Table 10-1. Factors supporting performance.

Factors Supporting Performance	Key Stakeholders
Clear performance specifications (expected outputs, standards)	Manager
Necessary support (funds, staff resources, priorities, responsibility, time)	Manager
Clear consequences (reinforcement, incentives, rewards, penalties)	Manager
Prompt feedback (how well performance matches expectations)	Manager
Individual capability (physical, mental, emotional capacity, experience)	Manager
Necessary skills and knowledge (adequate training, coaching, practice)	Manager, Trainer

SOURCE: Rummler, G., and A. Brache. (1995). *Improving Performance: How to Manage the White Space on the Organization Chart* (2d edition). San Francisco: Jossey-Bass.

organizations as systems, with inputs, processes, and outputs. A system can be defined as "a perceived whole whose elements 'hang together' because they continually affect each other over time and operate toward a common purpose" (Senge et al., 1994).

Wherever change is desired, key stakeholders must be identified and become involved to create a change-supporting environment in important system elements. All stakeholder efforts should be focused on supplying one or more of the six factors that support performance.

Identifying Key Stakeholders

As shown in table 10-1, the manager (from top executive to first-line manager, supervisor, or team leader) is a key stakeholder in providing all six factors that support performance. Individuals or groups in management roles must be closely involved in supporting any change effort. Note also that trainers or HPI professionals have a key role only in one factor: providing necessary knowledge and skills. They do, however, have a major role in educating all other stakeholders about their influence and responsibilities in all factors, to support full performance.

Who Are the Key Stakeholders?

Organizational systems depend on a mix of functions, components, and processes that result in specific products and services. The organization can be as simple as a roadside vegetable stand or as complex as a statewide mental health system. Who are the key stakeholders? They are the people who care about the results, contribute to the achievement of results, or both. In any organizational setting, key stakeholders may include but should not be limited to:

- managers
- learners
- HPI professionals
- co-workers
- HR professionals
- customers
- suppliers
- subject matter experts
- consultants
- union representatives
- community members
- advocacy groups
- government regulators.

Research Supporting Stakeholder Involvement

There is a growing body of research on the importance of involving stakeholders to support change, primarily in the area of transfer of learning. Much remains to be explored, but some important information has been determined. In the subsections that follow are summaries of four recent research studies on transfer to the job of skills gained in learning, a common type of performance improvement intervention. The studies' implications for transfer strategies, in supporting training interventions to achieve improved work performance, are shown as bulleted items. These strategies should also be considered for application in other types of HPI interventions besides training.

Management Signals of Transfer Importance

Baldwin and Magjuka (1991) surveyed typical learners to determine the indicators from managers at all levels that convinced learners that transfer of new skills was very important. The indicators are the following:

- Learners are held accountable for using the new knowledge and skills.
- The learning programs are mandatory, not left up to learners to choose.
- Managers give information before the training activity of the importance and need for transferring new knowledge and skills into performance.
- Managers demonstrate the importance of transfer by their personal involvement in the training activity, investing their own time and effort.

Pre- and Posttraining Discussions with Boss and Other Managerial Support

The importance of managers (or team leaders or other boss figures) giving prior information about the need to transfer new knowledge and skills as well as providing other support is demonstrated in research by Brinkerhoff and Montesino (1995). Learners in the treatment group reported significantly higher levels of skills application than did learners who did not have the following types of support:

- pre- and posttraining discussions with their bosses on the importance of the new knowledge and skills and how they are to be applied
- frequent practice opportunities to apply new skills
- clear indications that learners are held accountable for applying new learning.

Factors Distinguishing High-Performance Learners

There were significant differences between learners who rated themselves as high performers or low performers in a study by Feldstein and Boothman (1997). The researchers summarized their findings in six critical steps, three for learners and three for managers.

Learners should

- explore the subject matter before the training activity by reading and digging into the content

- develop clear ideas in advance on how to apply new skills
- practice new skills after the training activity.

Managers (including supervisors and team leaders) should

- communicate the importance of the three steps for learners and follow up to see that they are done
- develop and communicate clear performance expectations for learners after training
- develop and communicate how success will be measured.

Learners and Sponsors Bid for Training Opportunities

Seitz (1997) found significant increases in levels of transfer by learners when the learners and their sponsoring organizations had to bid for training opportunities. This, in effect, reverses the common practice in many organizations of the training function having to recruit learners to fill classes.

Systemic change (significantly greater than in previous experience) resulted after training when learners and sponsors in advance of training:

- analyzed their current and anticipated posttraining organizational environments
- identified potential improvements in organizational results that might be realized due to new skills to be gained in training
- specified transfer strategies by stakeholders that would be implemented to support successful application of new skills by learners
- identified measures of success for transfer of new skills to performance on the job (level 3 evaluation) and for important organizational results (level 4 evaluation).

Involving Stakeholders in the HPI Process

To emphasize the role of stakeholders throughout the HPI process, the HPI model is slightly modified in figure 10-1 to emphasize stakeholders and focus on organizational results.

Key stakeholders should be involved throughout the process for several purposes:

- to supply useful information from important perspectives on which to base decisions

- to participate in decision making
- to support buy-in of stakeholder groups in implementation of decisions.

Figure 10-1 also adds stages for stakeholder involvement in the determination of desired organizational results, actual organizational results, and the gap between the two. Results are the ultimate goal and determinant of organizational success, and stakeholders should be involved in determining and evaluating these as well.

Involvement of key stakeholders is absolutely critical at all stages of the change effort. Of course, all stakeholders won't be involved in everything; in some areas they have nothing to contribute and no interest in involvement. But the greater the involvement of stakeholders in areas they care about and can contribute to, the more support they can build for good decisions and their full implementation.

Identifying Stakeholder Strategies to Support Performance

When stakeholders come together to explore desired organizational results and the desired performance that will help produce those results, their basic tool is the list of factors that support performance (table 10-1). All stakeholders should become familiar with these factors, ensure that they are present in the work environment, and be able to refer to them in discussions of performance.

Stakeholders should determine what actions they can take to support one or more of the six factors supporting performance. These actions may include

- participation in the analysis of a performance improvement need and selection of an intervention
- involvement in design, delivery, and evaluation of the intervention
- support of communication about the importance of the intervention to other stakeholders
- provision of funding, subject matter experts, and other resources
- coaching and follow-up support after the intervention.

Figure 10-1. The HPI model with a central role for stakeholder involvement and a focus on organizational results.

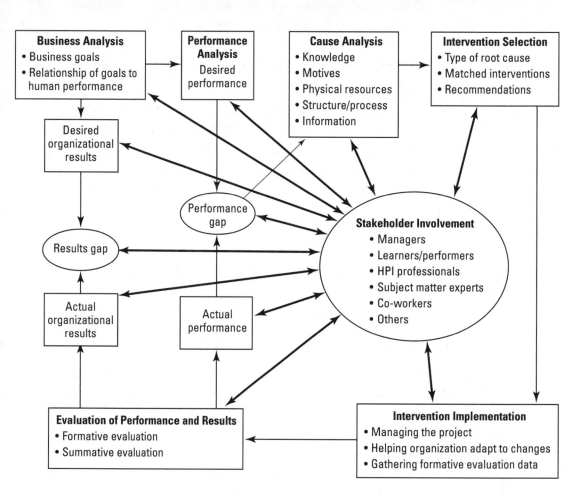

There is no single definitive list of transfer support actions appropriate to all organizations. Each organizational setting and its stakeholders are different and so are the requirements for each performance improvement intervention. A comprehensive list of generic stakeholder strategies, based on research, was included in what was perhaps the first book on the issue of transfer of learning (Broad & Newstrom, 1992). That list was used to suggest stakeholder strategies for the case provided later in this chapter on the Georgia Department of Human Resources's mental health initiative.

Many organizations have found a simple matrix of stakeholders and strategies to be a useful tool in developing and managing stakeholder activities to support an intervention. The basic matrix model is shown in table 10-2, organized around key stakeholders and three timeframes: before, during, and after an intervention. Of course, for interventions that are continuous, there may be no separate "after" timeframe. (For a specific example, see the matrix for the case study, table 10-3.)

A casebook, *In Action: Transferring Learning to the Workplace*, published by ASTD in 1997, presents 17 case studies of a wide range of organizations. The cases involved key stakeholders in HPI interventions (primarily learning activities). Each case shows a matrix of stakeholder interventions, tailored to

Table 10-2. Model of transfer strategies matrix.

Stakeholder	Before Intervention	During Intervention	After Intervention
Executive			
Manager			
Team Leader			
HPI professional			
Learner			
Co-worker			
Subject matter expert			
Other:			
Other:			

the specific organization and its performance challenge. This book can also be a useful reference for exploring possible stakeholder strategies for other HPI interventions in other organizational systems.

Identifying Evaluation Criteria

As the HPI model indicates, evaluation of outcomes is an essential part of the HPI process. (Chapter 11 covers evaluation in some detail.) Here, the emphasis is on involving stakeholders in several important aspects of the evaluation process:

- identifying criteria—before the intervention begins—by which success should be measured
- gathering baseline, formative, and summative evaluation data
- analyzing and drawing conclusions from the data
- taking actions to implement the conclusions
- communicating evaluation data to other stakeholders.

Criteria by which success will be measured should be identified before the intervention (such as training) is designed and implemented. Expanding on the HPI model, after the causes for the performance gap are identified, stakeholders should reach agreement on how the success of an intervention to eliminate that gap will be measured. This does not necessarily involve a complicated and expensive evaluation project. Depending on the desired outcomes, managers and other stakeholders may find some simple measures that will satisfy them. If possible, measures that the organization already collects should be used. Examples include sales, repeat sales, overall income, workforce attrition, waste, length and frequency of service center calls, billable hours, and number of returns.

Procedures for gathering data should be clear to all involved stakeholders before the intervention is implemented. If baseline data (before intervention) is important, it must be gathered at the appropriate time and in the right way. Other formative and summative data must be properly gathered and reported in a timely way to ensure the integrity of the evaluation process.

Stakeholders should contribute to the analysis to ensure their understanding of the evaluation data and their support for the conclusions reached. This will increase their commitment to take appropriate actions to act on conclusions and support improved performance.

Finally, stakeholders are the best communicators of evaluation data to their peers and other stakeholder groups. If they are convinced and committed to the conclusions reached, they are the most persuasive communicators of outcomes and results.

Case Study: Involving Stakeholders in Organizational Change

A complex organizational system is a collection of organizations, communities, groups, and individuals that are participants and stakeholders in varied interrelated input, process, and output activities to achieve a common goal. An example of just such a complex system is the mental health service system in the state of Georgia.

A Snapshot of the Organizational System

The Georgia Department of Human Resources, Division of Mental Health, Mental Retardation and Substance Abuse, supports the mental health service system throughout the state, the focus for this case study.

The system is very complex, including both public and private sector organizations in 13 regions, with salaried employees and volunteers, physicians and nurses, hospitals, clinics, and other care providers. Additional stakeholders include the governor and state legislature, researchers who produced the U.S. Surgeon General's 1999 report on mental health, local government officials, regional board members, owners and employees of contracted care provider organizations, several advocacy organizations, consumers who are the ultimate users of the system's products and services, their family members, the criminal justice and school systems, and community groups of various types. Outputs of the system include delivery of mental health services to individual consumers, their families, hospitals, nursing homes, and other entities. An attempt to portray this complex system resulted in the diagram in figure 10-2.

Best Practices Into Best Services

For some years, the Division had sponsored an annual best practices conference to present research results and other best practices information to people in many organizations and groups throughout the state. This conference had traditionally focused on one clinical best practice theme.

Figure 10-2. Georgia's mental health delivery system.

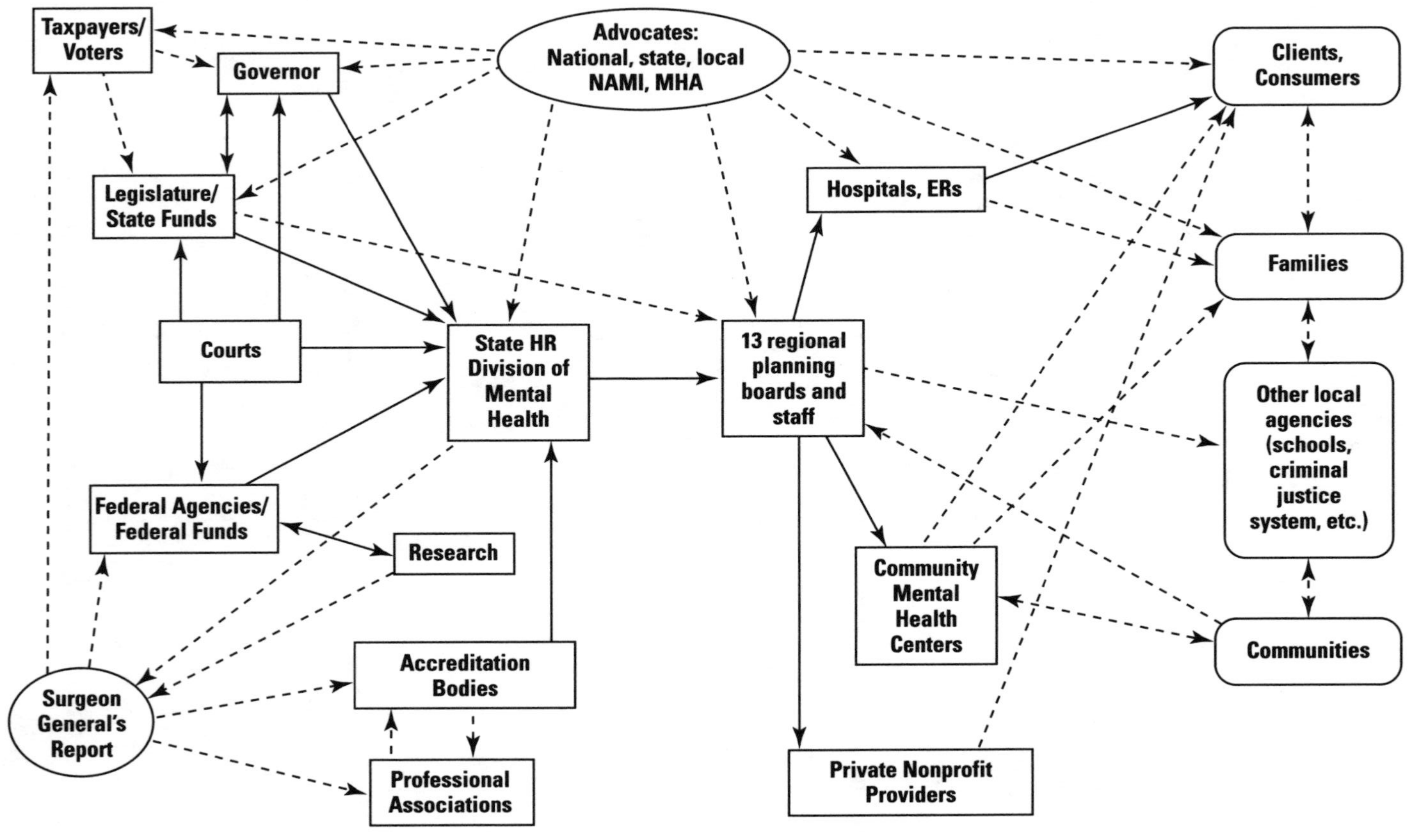

Solid lines indicate line or contractual authority; dashed lines indicate influence, not authority. This diagram is still evolving and is not a final view of the system.

While planning for the 1999 conference, the medical director (Thomas W. Hester, M.D.) learned that the first *U.S. Surgeon General's Report on Mental Health* was about to be released. He encouraged planners to take advantage of this important event as they chose a conference theme. Most of the best practices expected to be named in the report had already been conference themes. Yet, these best practices had not become standard practice in Georgia. Anticipating release of the Surgeon General's report, the 1999 conference focused entirely on implementation strategies to help Georgia's mental health service system turn best practice concepts into best practice services for consumers.

The shift in emphasis from clinical practices to the management practice of implementation was very well received by conference attendees. With this in mind, the conference planners decided to redirect conference resources from producing an annual conference in 2000 and 2001 to more fully developing implementation skills in the system. The result was a Learning Transfer plan to assist regions in implementing at least one of the best practices of the Surgeon General's report during the 2002 fiscal year.

A series of regional workshops was presented in September 2000 to orient the regional boards and others to the Learning Transfer plan and its requirements and benefits. All requirements for participation in the plan were carefully integrated into the existing work cycle of the regions. The project provides an experienced facilitator, trained in learning transfer concepts, to assist each region individually in selecting a best practice and developing a plan for learning transfer with key stakeholders. As an incentive for participation, the provider that gets the contract to deliver the service receives free clinical training in the skills and knowledge necessary to deliver the specific best practice.

How the Learning Transfer Program Is Working

As the program evolved, several regions worked with facilitators to select an appropriate best practice from the Surgeon General's report; develop a learning transfer project appropriate to the region; and involve stakeholders in design, delivery, and evaluation of the new programs. Most learning transfer projects involve clinical training for care providers (physicians, nurses, social workers, community health workers, and consumers of mental health services) in delivering the best practice services. Examples of these clinical best practices (each requiring some sort of improved performance by care providers) include the following:

- Assertive Community Treatment (ACT) teams (provision of comprehensive care in the community by an interdisciplinary team of case managers, psychiatrist, nurses, social workers, and others)

- peer support programs focused on consumer recovery (including consumer-operated drop-in centers and peer-led initiatives within existing programs)

- new generation medications (increased use of more effective medications, based on recent pharmacological research).

To assist regions and facilitators in planning for clinical training in one of the best practices, the manager of the Learning Transfer project for the Division (Jeanette Edwards Lewis) created a generic learning transfer matrix that could be adapted to any specific clinical training (table 10-3). This matrix assumes that stakeholders include the clinical director, various program managers, staff members, and the trainer. Additional stakeholders can be identified for a specific best practice. (For example, for an ACT team program, representatives of local criminal justice and public housing systems might be included.) This matrix is quite generic and is readily adaptable to other organizational learning requirements and HPI interventions in additional settings.

Because Georgia's Learning Transfer project is still in its early stages, no evaluation data is yet available. Inevitably, as in any complex system, some of the original players have moved on to other situations, and new players have picked up their responsibilities. The ultimate measures of success will be increased application throughout the state's mental health delivery system of clinical best practices as outlined in the Surgeon General's report.

Table 10-3. Generic learning transfer matrix.

Stakeholder	Before Clinical Training	During Clinical Training	After Clinical Training
Clinical Director	• Emphasize new performance goals for organization • Establish baseline performance data • Talk up the training • Establish transfer of training in performance standards of supervisors	• Introduce trainer on site • Talk up training initiative to all staff outside training	• Regularly monitor status of transfer strategies by all stakeholders • Assess changes in performance data

Stakeholder	Before Clinical Training	During Clinical Training	After Clinical Training
Program Managers	• Involve staff in performance gap analysis and training needs assessment • Review training content and select parts needed by staff • Establish skills to be learned as measurable expectations in performance reviews • Brief learners on content, importance, performance objectives, and process of training • Provide time to complete pre-course assignments	• Prevent interruptions during training • Attend training with staff • Look for opportunities to recognize accomplishments, good thinking, etc., in class discussions • Monitor attendance	• Plan reentry of learners to work after training to overcome inertia of prior routine • Keep the focus on new performance by scheduling updates and anecdotes of success at each staff meeting * Regularly attend and assign staff to attend staff meetings of other programs involved in new performance
Learners (Staff Members)	• Participate actively in performance gap analysis, training needs assessment, and development of learning transfer strategies by stakeholders • Complete precourse assignments	• Show up ready to learn and participate • Ask real-life application questions • Keep "ideas and applications" notebook • Develop individual action plan to use new skills • Anticipate "relapse" and plan how to avoid it	• Implement individual action plan • Practice self-management of new performance • Maintain contact and share ideas with staff in other programs who shared training • Participate in evaluations of performance outcomes
Trainer	• Provide on-site coordinator with training title, content, objectives, schedule, on-site setting requirements, and list of materials/texts to be ordered prior to training • Provide precourse readings • Specify data needed to use in "real" practice exercises • Submit "teaching methods" plan to Division, which contracts with trainer, to ensure appropriate transfer strategies are used by trainer • Coach program manager on selection of staff	• Systematically design or modify predesigned training to meet needs of particular group being trained • Use strategies to promote transfer of learning (job-related exercises, job aids, individual action plans, etc.)	• Schedule regular telephone contact with program managers to troubleshoot, coach, and congratulate on new performance successes • Refer program managers to literature, other clinical staff • Email information and reminders to learners about key issues and programs

(continued next page)

Table 10-3. Generic learning transfer matrix. *(continued)*

Stakeholder	Before Clinical Training	During Clinical Training	After Clinical Training
Other Stakeholders	• Participate in performance gap analysis and training needs assessment • Talk up the training goals • Plan participation in training as appropriate	• Attend parts of training as appropriate • Encourage learners to share learning • Provide support to clinical director and program managers as appropriate	• Comment on new performance achievements • Participate in evaluation of outcomes as appropriate • Publicize new performance in community as appropriate

Source: Lewis, J.E. (2001). Georgia Department of Human Resources, Division of Mental Health, Mental Retardation and Substance Abuse.

Summary

This chapter has discussed the role and importance of stakeholders in achieving and maintaining desired performance change in organizations. The most obvious stakeholders in performance improvement are managers at all levels, the performers themselves, and HPI professionals involved in the effort. Additional stakeholders should also be involved in areas in which they have both interests and leverage to affect the change process.

You, as an HPI professional, are the stakeholder in the best position to help the organization determine the desired change, identify key stakeholders, select the appropriate interventions, educate stakeholders on their essential roles in supporting transfer, evaluate progress, and continue and maintain the change process. You can educate other stakeholders about the research on support for performance change and their responsibilities and leverage. Using the matrix tool provided in this chapter, you can manage and track the strategies those stakeholders use to influence change.

Building support for stakeholder involvement in lasting performance change allows you, as an HPI professional, to become a valued partner with organizational decision makers. The rewards for this partnership are great in increased recognition for your accomplishments and in the satisfaction of seeing effective and measurable performance change take place.

Your HPI Challenge

To help you apply transfer principles to your own practice, consider the following.

✓ First, think of some performance by someone—an individual or group—that you would like to see changed (improved or established). This could be performance related to your job or work environment, to some community issue or activity, or to your family.

_____

_____

✓ Now, consider who are the stakeholders in that performance. Look at the list of stakeholders that appeared in this chapter and consider who might have some interest in the performance you are focusing on. (Don't forget that the performer is a key stakeholder!) If your focus is on performance in a complex system, consider some of the additional stakeholders in the Georgia mental health complex system (figure 10-2), because these may trigger some ideas for other stakeholders in your system.

_____

_____

✓ With key stakeholders in mind, take a look at the six factors supporting performance (table 10-1). To what extent is each of those factors fully in place to support the desired performance you have in mind? (Usually, several factors need additional support.) Which stakeholders are in a position to supply the needed factors?

_____

_____

_____

_____

_____

✓ Now, contact all key stakeholders to confirm their interest in the performance you are focusing on. If possible, pull them all together to work collaboratively through the entire HPI process (figure 10-1). Be sure that the stakeholders you work with have decision-making authority to commit to strategies to support the desired performance.

References

Baldwin, T., and R. Magjuka. (Spring, 1991). "Organizational Training and Signals of Importance." *Human Resource Development Quarterly,* 25–36.

Brinkerhoff, R., and M. Montesino. (Fall, 1995). "Partnerships for Training Transfer." *Human Resource Development Quarterly,* 263–274.

Broad, M., editor. (1997). *In Action: Transferring Learning to the Workplace.* Alexandria, VA: ASTD.

Broad, M., and J. Newstrom. (1992). *Transfer of Training: Action-Packed Strategies to Ensure High Payoff from Training Investments.* Reading, MA: Addison-Wesley.

Csoka, L. (1994). *Closing the Human Performance Gap.* Research Report, 1065–94–RR. New York: The Conference Board.

Feldstein, H., and T. Boothman. (1997). "Success Factors in Technology Training." *In Action: Transferring Learning to the Workplace.* Alexandria, VA: ASTD.

Robinson, D.G., and J.C. Robinson (editors). (1998). *Moving From Training to Performance: A Practical Guidebook.* Alexandria, VA: ASTD and Berrett-Koehler.

Senge, P., R. Ross, B. Smith, C. Roberts, and A. Kleiner. (1994). *The Fifth Discipline Fieldbook: Strategies and Tools for Building a Learning Organization.* New York: Currency Doubleday.

Seitz, S. (1997). "Transfer Strategies for Communities: Substance Abuse Prevention." *In Action: Transferring Learning to the Workplace.* Alexandria, VA: ASTD.

Additional Resources

JHPIEGO Corporation and Prime II Project. (2002). *Transfer of Learning: A Guide for Strengthening the Performance of Health Care Workers.* http://www.reproline.jhu.edu/english/6read/6pi/tol/index.htm.

Rummler, G., and A. Brache. (1995). *Improving Performance: How to Manage the White Space on the Organization Chart* (2d edition). San Francisco: Jossey-Bass.

About the Author

Mary Broad helps organizations achieve high workforce performance through strategic planning, performance analysis, and instructional design and delivery. She is widely published on strategies to ensure full transfer of learning to performance. Broad has presented in the United States, Canada, Indonesia, Ireland, Kuwait, Mexico, Singapore, and South Korea. Recent clients include Pfizer Pharmaceuticals, L.G. Electronics, Groupe INSEP, U.S. Food and Drug Administration, U.S. Marshals Service, and the National Academy of Public Administration. She may be contacted via email at marybroad@earthlink.net.

Evaluation: Was Your HPI Project Worth the Effort?

Holly Burkett

Key Points

> ➤ Evaluation data is needed not only to validate HPI work, but also to gain support and cooperation for implementing it.

> ➤ Human performance improvement professionals cannot expect to improve and measure the performance of an organization without first evaluating their own knowledge, capacity, and motives around performance measurement and evaluation.

> ➤ The role of the evaluator is to identify the impact of an intervention on individual or organizational effectiveness.

> ➤ To ensure staff commitment to the process, it's important to emphasize the purpose of evaluation in terms of a continuous improvement strategy and not a source of performance measurement for staff.

> ➤ A sound evaluation plan, especially at level 5 (return-on-investment), must include a method to isolate the effects of the program from other influences.

> ➤ Not all interventions are candidates for a level 4 or 5 evaluation.

> ➤ Communicating results is as important as achieving them.

➤ Integrating evaluation into the performance improvement process requires a framework in which evaluation strategies are linked throughout the cause analysis, design, and delivery stages of the HPI intervention.

Despite heightened interest in HPI measurement and increased account-ability to prove bottom-line value, many practitioners are deterred from sys-tematic evaluation efforts because of fears or myths associated with the com-plexity and cost of implementing the process. Some HPI professionals even argue that measuring business results of an HPI intervention isn't possible. Yet in a business climate demanding faster, cheaper solutions to complex performance problems, the ability to create expedient, multifaceted, and credi-ble evaluation systems is critical. How can you know if you've matched the right solution to the right problem without some form of evaluation and measurement?

Consider the primary purposes and use of evaluation:

- to determine if a program or intervention is accomplishing its objectives
- to determine if the performance gap was closed or narrowed
- to determine if the intervention met the intended business goals
- to determine the benefit-cost ratio of an HPI or HRD program

---

Why Interventions Fail

Consider these common reasons that HPI solutions fail to add value:

- Solutions are not linked specifically to strategies, challenges, or prob-lems in the organization.
- Solutions focus on individuals and not operating units.
- Participants attend HPI programs for reasons other than personal or organizational need.
- Performance improvement programs are not aligned with partici-pants' daily work environment.
- Immediate supervisors do not support or reinforce learners' on-the-job application of learned skills or knowledge.

- to provide data for decision making about expanding or discontinuing programs.

Evaluation is also a way of connecting business performance outcomes with the inputs, outputs, and processes of an HPI intervention, along with showing the benefits of those results in comparison to the costs of the intervention itself. For practitioners tasked with improving organizational performance, it's important to assess whether the cost of closing the performance gap is greater than the cost of allowing the gap to continue. In short, well-managed, well-documented, and well-communicated evaluation data is needed not only to validate HPI work, but also to gain support and cooperation for implementing it.

Evaluation: The Fifth Level

Kirkpatrick (1998) created a four-level model of categorizing evaluation data that has been used as a common frame of reference for several decades (see chapter 1). Phillips (1997) expanded upon this framework to incorporate a fifth level of evaluation for capturing the financial impact of HPI programs: return-on-investment, or ROI (table 11-1). Many impact studies stop at a report of business results at level 4 and consider a program a success if it produces business enhancements in such areas as quality, call volume, or satisfaction. That information is important, but the ultimate level of evaluation shows how the costs of the program compare to the value of the result.

Table 11-1. Phillips's five-level framework for evaluation.

Level	Measures
1. Reaction and Planned Action	Participant's reaction to the program and outlines specific plans for implementation
2. Learning	Skills, knowledge, or attitude changes
3. Application	Changes in behavior on the job and specific application of the training material
4. Business Impact	Business impact of the program
5. ROI	Monetary value of the results and costs for the program, usually expressed as a percentage

Level 5 evaluation measures how the monetary benefits of the program compare with the costs of the program. Two common formulas for calculating the actual return are the benefit-cost ratio (BCR) and ROI. For calculating the BCR, you divide the total benefits of the program by the program costs:

$$BCR = \text{Total Benefits} \div \text{Program Costs}$$

To calculate ROI, the program costs are subtracted from the total benefits to produce the net benefits, which are then divided by the costs.

$$ROI\ (\%) = \frac{\text{Net Benefits}}{\text{Program Costs}} \times 100$$

Professional and Personal Perspectives on Evaluation

Who's going to invest in an HPI initiative that can't prove its value? The promise of HPI is that there will be verifiable positive results by using a scientific and systemic approach to performance improvement. Yet, many HPI professionals resist systemic measures of an intervention's benefits, analysis of its verifiable, tangible results, and implementation of ROI strategies because of beliefs that it takes away from the human side of performance.

In HPI work, human behavior is often measured in terms of an individual's knowledge, capacity, and motive. The same components apply to the HPI practitioner's behavioral use of evaluation methods. In other words, it's important to recognize that the HPI professional cannot expect to improve and measure the performance of an organization without first evaluating his or her own knowledge, capacity, and motives around performance measurement and evaluation.

If it is assumed that there is a link between learners' attitudes and performance, then it must also be assumed that the same link exists for practitioners. Subsequently, achieving a results-oriented evaluation approach begins with the mindset and philosophy of the HPI team. How do you think about evaluation? How do you plan for it, implement it, use it? How much time are you willing to spend on evaluation? How do you rank evaluation on your list of priorities?

There are other compelling reasons to apply evaluation strategies to your own HPI work:

- *Business understanding:* If you don't understand what measures management is using, how can you expect to affect those measures?
- *Economic sense:* Evaluation makes good economic sense and should be required of any activity that represents a significant expenditure of funds.
- *Budget approval:* In a cost-competitive climate where budget approval is constrained, HPI professionals need to provide solid measurements of a past programs' successes to secure additional funds for the future.
- *Survival:* Like it or not, the accountability issue is here to stay. Increased pressure from the top to show value-added contributions will remain a driving force in HPI practice.
- *Rising evaluation standards:* Pressure from other HPI professionals who have contributed to the growing literature of ROI case study and research applications continues to raise the bar in evaluation performance standards.
- *Self-satisfaction:* This is the satisfaction of knowing and articulating your bottom-line contribution and demonstrating that your efforts make a difference to your organization.
- *Professionalism:* Evaluation skill sets are a core competency associated with the evaluator role in HPI work (Rothwell, 1996). In addition, part of any profession is to show the worth of its function.

Evaluation Lingo

It is helpful to embark on evaluation with a foundation in the terminology. Table 11-2 offers some definitions of terms that you are likely to encounter.

Planning Your Evaluation

In making the transition from a traditional reactive evaluation process to a more systemic and results-based effort, it's important to dispel the myth that evaluation is an add-on process occurring at the end of a program. Integrating evaluation into the HPI process requires a framework in which evaluation strategies are linked throughout the cause analysis, design, and delivery stages of the HPI intervention. This framework requires significant planning.

Table 11-2. Common evaluation and measurement terms.

Term	Definition
Content validity	Measures how well a test represents key samples of the knowledge, skill, or performance areas being tested.
Construct validity	Refers to the degree to which an instrument accurately measures the targeted concepts it's meant to measure (e.g., efficiency, listening skill).
Control group and experimental group	The experimental group participates in the HPI intervention; the control group of participants, who are as similar as possible to those in the experimental group, is not involved in the intervention.
Criterion-related validity—predictive	Refers to how well a test score predicts future performance in the area tested.
Criterion-related validity—concurrent	Refers to the extent in which a test agrees with the results of other measures or instruments given at approximately the same time to measure like characteristics.
Gap	Difference between actual and desired performance.
Hard data	Performance measures that are generally grouped into four categories of output, quality, cost, and time.
Inputs	The resources (i.e., information, material, people, process outputs) used to perform a job or task.
Outcomes	The effects of the outputs upon such areas as cost, quality, satisfaction, and time.
Outputs	The product of the work process(es).
Quantity	Refers to the number of items or tasks during a fixed period.
Quality	Describes characteristics of the product or service that meet specifications.
Reliability	A reliable instrument is one that is consistent enough that subsequent measurements of an item give approximately the same results.
Sampling	A method used to decide the characteristics and the size of the group(s) of individuals who will participate in the evaluation.
Soft data	Behaviorally based and often difficult to measure accurately or assign dollar values to. Categories include work habits, new skills, work climate, development, advancement, feelings, attitudes, and initiative.

Term	Definition
Time	Refers to the time to produce a single item or complete a single task or project, seconds or months.
Validity	Probably the most important characteristic of an evaluation instrument is validity. A valid instrument measures what the person using the instrument wishes to measure. The degree to which it performs this function satisfactorily is called relative validity.
Unit of work performance	Often a focal point in performance measurement with primary emphasis on dimensions of time, quantity, and quality. Examples include items produced and time required to complete a project.
Variables	Levers in an organization that influence performance, including available tools, organizational culture, policies, and incentives.

Assume that every intervention succeeds because of proper planning and that the best way to add value is to know what you're doing and where you're going. The following guidelines will help you get started planning your own evaluation.

Establish an Evaluation Framework. The framework provides your road-map for conducting evaluation and allows you to begin with the end in mind. For purposes of this chapter, Phillips's ROI model (1997) will be used to show a proven, step-by-step process for collecting data across all five levels, isolating the effects of a performance improvement program, converting data to monetary value, and identifying the intangible benefits of an HPI intervention. The model (figure 11-1) emphasizes that the process is a continuous flow from one step to the next.

Develop a Data Collection Plan. Data collection is the focal point of the ROI process and needs to be addressed from the beginning. It is imperative to use a variety of methods to collect data. Recognize that each program, target audience, and situation is different. In some environments, focus groups, action plans, and questionnaires work well, and, in others, performance monitoring and performance contracts are better suited. Get input and management approval for your sampling approach. And, be sure to take staff expertise, evaluation resources, and type of program into account as you create a data collection plan.

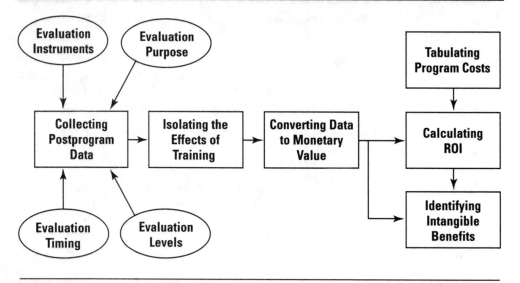

Figure 11-1. Phillips's ROI model for collecting level 5 evaluation data.

SOURCE: Phillips, J.J. (1997). *Return on Investment in Training and Performance Improvement Programs.* Houston: Gulf Publishing.

The data you collect should be directly related to and integrated into the HPI objectives identified during the needs analysis process. The objectives provide the link between the gap or needs analysis and the evaluation process. Here are some guidelines for defining objectives at all evaluation levels, as defined by Phillips:

- Level 1 (reaction and planned action) objectives define the expected reaction and planned action from the participants.

- Level 2 (learning) objectives identify the specific knowledge and skill measures targeted for learning and enhanced performance.

- Level 3 (application) objectives identify the measurable, observable performance expected back on the job after the intervention is completed and participants apply what they have learned. These objectives are critical because they describe expected outcomes and levels of proficiency that should result from the HPI or HRD intervention. As such, they must be well worded and specific to measurable and observable behaviors. Phillips recommends that these key questions be asked when developing application objectives: What new or improved knowledge will be applied on the job? What new or improved skill will be applied on the job? What is the frequency of skill application? What new tasks will be performed (initiated, maintained, increased, modified)? What new steps or action items will be implemented? What new processes will be implemented or changed? Finally, level 3 objectives provide a foundation for level 4 evaluation and enable the HPI staff to assess the extent to which environmental barriers may have prevented application or transfer.

- Level 4 (business results) objectives identify measures of business impact influenced by the program or intervention. For example, if one of the objectives were to improve quality, specific quality measures (for example, minutes of downtime or defects per thousand units produced) would be included.

- Level 5 (ROI) objectives identify the desired BCR or ROI. Many organizations target ROI goals based upon the value of other investments, although others may strive just to break even. Remember, ROI analysis is a continuation of data collection planning. For best results, use a variety of data collection methods.

Although business results and ROI may be desired, evaluation at the other levels needs to occur in order to show a chain of impact (Phillips, 1997). In other words, as skills and knowledge are learned (level 2) and then applied or transferred back to the job (level 3), they then produce business results (level 4) that may or not produce a positive return (level 5).

All four elements of evaluation—purpose, levels, tools, and timing—need to be considered when developing a data collection plan. By planning early for data collection, there is clear direction as to what type of data will be collected, how it will be collected, when it will be collected, and who will collect it. Ideally, the data collection plan should be completed prior to the launch of a new training program, immediately after the preliminary information is gathered and the program's evaluation targets are selected.

Establishing an Evaluation Purpose. Although evaluation is usually viewed as a component of continuous improvement for the HPI process, it's important to identify distinct purposes for evaluation planning. These include

- determining if a program or intervention is accomplishing its objectives
- finding out if the human performance gap was closed or narrowed
- gauging the extent of transfer to the job and identifying barriers and enablers to transfer

- assessing improvement areas in the needs assessment and the program or intervention
- calculating the BCR of an HPI or HRD program
- providing data for decision making about expanding or discontinuing programs.

To ensure staff commitment to the process, it's important to emphasize that evaluation is a continuous improvement strategy and not a means of performance measurement for staff.

Setting Evaluation Levels or Targets. Not every program is a candidate for a level 4 or 5 evaluation. Some organizations set evaluation targets that describe the percentage of programs that will be measured at each level. Just as your evaluation framework provides a roadmap, your evaluation targets provide a compass with which to set direction and maintain focus.

For example, a one-person HRD department at a manufacturing facility may perform level 1 evaluations on 100 percent of interventions, but a level 4 or 5 evaluation may be carried out on only 10 percent of its interventions. How do you choose which programs should be subjected to level 4 or 5 evaluation? Suggested selection criteria include the life cycle of the program, how critical the program is in terms of business needs, the program's cost and visibility in the organization, the number of learners who are affected, and the importance of the program to senior management.

Developing Evaluation Instruments. A variety of instruments can be used to collect evaluation data. The appropriate instruments should be considered in the early stages of ROI development and should connect to your evaluation purpose. The seven most common instruments are

1. surveys
2. questionnaires
3. interviews
4. focus groups
5. tests
6. observations
7. performance records.

When designing or using an evaluation instrument, be clear about the information needed; test the proposed questions for understanding; address the anonymity issue; and consider ease of use, tabulation, and analysis.

Evaluation Timing. In this aspect of the process, it's important to consider and communicate the timing for follow-up evaluation. Some situations may require the use of pre- and postintervention measurements, and others may not have those measures available. Follow-up with action plan implementation is usually conducted three weeks after the program, whereas follow-up with questionnaires and surveys can range from two to six months later.

Evaluation of an HPI Intervention: A Case Study

This case describes an ROI study of a pilot process improvement team deployed as an HPI strategy for increasing operational efficiency in a dynamic manufacturing environment. Methodologies included an intensive training program with specific application (level 3) and business results (level 4) objectives based upon identified needs, a competency instrument to measure learning objectives (level 2), action planning to measure on-the-job behavior (level 3), impact questionnaires with the use of estimates to isolate program effects, and data analysis of historical data to evaluate business impact and ROI (level 5). This study was awarded a select International Society for Performance Improvement (ISPI) research grant and was conducted in accordance with ISPI guidelines for human performance technology research.

Figure 11-2 is a completed data collection plan with identified objectives, methodologies, and timing for each targeted level of evaluation carried out for this case study.

The evaluation covered the following targets:

- *Reaction:* Level 1 data was collected at the end of the program and solicited again during the 30-day impact questionnaire process. Project sponsor and steering committee reaction was also collected through an impact questionnaire at the end of the project.
- *Learning:* Level 2 data was measured during the intervention with pre- and postprogram self-assessments and through behavior observation during skill practice and training review activities. This

Figure 11-2. Example of a data collection plan for a process improvement team.

Program: *BETA Process Improvement Team*   **Responsibility:** *Training and Development*

Date: _____

Evaluation Level	Objective(s)	Data Collection Method	Data Sources	Timing	Responsibilities
1 **Reaction**	• To measure participant satisfaction with process improvement training • To identify recommendations for improvement in instructional design • To identify recommendations for improvement in linkage of program objectives to business needs	• Reaction questionnaire • Impact questionnaire	• Participants • Managers, supervisors • Steering committee	• After each session • During session • 30, 60 days	• Training and development consultant • Participants
2 **Learning**	• To measure participants' learning gains with process improvement learning objectives	• Skill practice exercises, simulations • Qualification instrument	• Participants • Training consultant	• During session • Before/during • One week after	• Participants • Training and development consultant
3 **Application**	• To measure participants' application of process improvement performance objectives • To measure frequency and relevance of use • To identify barriers in applying learned skills/knowledge	• Individual action plans • Team project follow-up session(s) • Impact questionnaire	• Participants • Steering committee • Supervisors • Line personnel affected by project actions	• During action plan implementation • two months after program	• Training and development consultant • Project sponsor • Steering committee • Participants • Participants' supervisors
4 **Business Results**	• To measure extent to which applied skills/knowledge affected strategic goal of increasing configure-to-order (CTO) capacity	• Performance monitoring of BETA line • Impact questionnaire	• Steering committee • Production recorder data • Participants	• two months after action plan implementation	• Training and development consultant • Subject matter experts • Participants
5 **ROI**	• To measure ROI for HPI strategy • To measure benefits-to-cost ratio	• BCR analysis • Impact questionnaire	• Participants • Production data • Units per person per hour and labor cost conversions	• two months after action plan completion • three months after program	• Training and development consultant • Subject matter experts

SOURCE: Adapted with permission from J.J. Phillips, Jack Phillips Center for Research.1999.

target included a corresponding qualification or competency instrument with critical knowledge and skill sets linked to core performance objectives.

- *Application:* Level 3 data—on-the-job behavior change—was monitored and measured by implementing an action plan (figure 11-3). This simple approach captures data about how participants plan to apply specific skills and knowledge from the program, as well as the projected monetary value of these planned actions to the organization. Impact questionnaires (figure 11-4) were used to gauge learners' perceptions about applying their learning on the job.

- *Business results:* Level 4 data was evaluated by using expert formulas for efficiency measures and by comparing the targeted line's performance against those measures for the 60 days before and after HPI implementation. Another source of level 4 data was participant/expert estimates of potential cost benefits associated with both applied behaviors and identified business improvements. This data was collected in the 30- and 60-day impact questionnaires, which sought information about the cost benefits, the level of confidence that respondents had in their estimates, and barriers to applying the new behavior.

- *ROI:* Level 5 data was captured using the job aid in figure 11-5, a sample ROI analysis plan.

Calculating ROI for the Intervention

To calculate ROI, the program costs were tabulated and fully loaded to include analysis costs, development costs, delivery costs, and evaluation costs. Another important factor is intangible benefits, the sixth data measure in Phillips's model of ROI evaluation, and, for some programs, the most important. Intangible benefits are those benefits that have not been converted to monetary value, such as increased morale, improved teamwork, or increased job satisfaction. Figure 11-6 shows all program costs, program benefits (tangible and intangible), and the calculations used to derive ROI for the HPI intervention.

This case study illustrates a very conservative approach to ROI calculation and shows the importance of basing results on calculations accepted by senior management. In this example, the initial calculation of monetary benefits associated with increased labor efficiency was arbitrarily adjusted

Figure 11-3. Model action plan for continuous improvement training program.

Name _____ Instructor Signature _____ Follow-up Date _____

Objective To apply skills and knowledge from Continuous Improvement Program   Evaluation Period _____ to _____

Improvement Measures: (Productivity, Labor Efficiency/Downtime, Process Failures, Rework, Customer Response, Communication, Cycle Time, Other)

Action Step	Analysis

As a result of this program, what specific actions will you apply based upon what you have learned?
 	
1. _____
   _____
   _____
   _____
2. _____
   _____
   _____
3. _____
   _____
   _____
4. _____
   _____
   _____
 	
Comments: _____
	What specific unit of measure will change as a result of your actions?
	
	1. _____
	   _____
	   _____
	2. _____
	   _____
	3. As a result of the anticipated changes in the above, please *estimate* the monetary benefits to your department.
	   $ _____
	4. What is the basis of your estimate?
	   _____
	   _____
	5. What level of confidence, expressed as a percentage, do you place on the above estimate? (100% = Certainty and 0% = No Confidence)
	   _____ %
	6. What other factors, besides training, may contribute to benefits associated with process improvements changes?
	   _____
	7. What barriers, if any, may prevent you from using skills or knowledge gained from this program? _____
	   _____

Intangible Benefits: _____
_____
_____

SOURCE: Adapted with permission from J.J. Phillips, Jack Phillips Center for Research. 1999.

Figure 11-4. Examples of application questions for learners.

Listed below are the performance objectives from the continuous improvement training project. After reflecting on this training one month later, please use the following scale to circle the degree to which you have (a) applied the following skills and knowledge in your job; and (b) the degree to which application of skills and knowledge has improved your effectiveness on the job.

Scale	1	2	3	4	5
Frequency of Application	Rarely (once a month)	Seldom (once every 2 weeks)	Occasionally (1–2 times a week)	Frequently (once a day)	Very frequently (several times a day)
Improved Job Effectiveness	Not much improvement	Somewhat improved	Moderately improved	Definitely improved	Significantly improved

Performance Objective(s)	Frequency	Effectiveness
a. Apply a common language for communicating about process issues	1 2 3 4 5	1 2 3 4 5
b. Define customer requirements in a work process	1 2 3 4 5	1 2 3 4 5
c. Analyze a work process, using continuous improvement tools provided	1 2 3 4 5	1 2 3 4 5
d. Identify weak links or bottlenecks in a work process	1 2 3 4 5	1 2 3 4 5
e. Demonstrate consensus-building skills in problem solving and decision making	1 2 3 4 5	1 2 3 4 5
f. Increase capability to meet build-to-order (BTO) or configure-to-order (CTO) requirements	1 2 3 4 5	1 2 3 4 5

and cut in half by the project steering committee, which determined that the initial estimates were subjective and not sufficiently conservative. Participants and subject matter experts had actually calculated a 314 percent ROI for the continuous improvement intervention.

Outcomes of the Intervention

The senior management team was pleased with the outcome of this program and, in particular, by the tangible business results that showed more

Figure 11-5. Example ROI analysis plan.

Program: BETA Continuous Improvement   **Team Responsibility:** Training and Development   **Date:** _____

Data Items (Usually Level 4)	Methods for Isolating the Effects of the Program/Process	Methods to Convert Data to Monetary Values	Cost Categories	Intangible Benefits	Communication Targets for Final Report	Other Influences/ Issues During Application
Level 4 CTO capacity	Participant estimates Subject matter expert estimates	Historical data Subject matter expert formulas Performance monitoring of targeted line	Assessment costs Design costs Delivery, facilitation costs Participant salaries and benefits Steering Committee salaries and benefits	Satisfaction Productivity Communication Teamwork Problem solving and decision making Systems thinking	Steering Committee Program participants and their supervisors HR and development staff Line staff affected by reengineering effort	Management support Engineering support Training support New product ramps Attrition Moving targets Resistance to change
Level 5 Labor cost per unit per person UPPH	Participant estimates Subject matter expert estimates	Direct conversion using production recorder data and engineering formulas for labor costs, UPPH costs, product life cycles	Evaluation costs			

SOURCE: Adapted with permission from J.J. Phillips, Jack Phillips Center for Research. 1999.

Figure 11-6. Example ROI calculation for the case study intervention.

Target Group

Pilot groups of cross-functional team members in a dynamic manufacturing environment

HPI Intervention Methods

- Customized continuous improvement training program
- Job performer competency assessments
- Work redesign
- Reengineering of material flow

Impact Objectives

- Increase operational capacity in meeting configure-to-order requirements
- Increase output of units per person per hour
- Increase labor efficiency

Collection Methods

- Level 1 data: Reaction survey, impact questionnaire
- Level 2 data: Pre/postassessments, competency assessment, skill practice observations
- Level 3 data: 30-, 60-day impact questionnaire; individual action plans; performance monitoring
- Level 4 data: Participant, supervisor, and expert estimates; production data on targeted line's performance

Isolating the Effects of the Program

- Participant, supervisor, expert estimates
- Forecasting

Program Costs

- Fully loaded to include analysis costs; development costs; participant salaries and benefits, delivery costs; and evaluation costs
- Total program cost: $53,000 (rounded)

Intangible Benefits

- Increased systems view
- Increased problem-solving skills
- Improved cross-functional collaboration
- Improved decision making
- Improved process understanding
- Better picture of the cost associated with production

ROI Calculation

Monetary benefits from increased UPPH

- Value of labor cost per unit = $7.42
- Value of increase in units per person per hour = 5%
- Value of labor cost benefit per person per unit =
    $7.42 \times .05 = .37$
- Number of average units per week =
    $10,000 \times .37 = \$3,700$
- Value of average product life cycle =
    $\$3,700 \times 21.5 \text{ weeks} = \$79,550$

Monetary benefits from increased labor efficiency

- Estimated value of labor efficiency increase = $70,058 (50% of $140,116 per steering committee adjustment factor)
- Benefits = $79,550 + $70,058 = $149,608

$$ROI (\%) = \frac{\text{Net Program Benefits}}{\text{Program Costs}} \times 100$$

$$ROI = \frac{\$149,608 - \$53,000 \text{ (Program Costs)}}{\$53,000} = 1.82 \times 100 = 182\%$$

configured-to-order products being built more quickly. It was uniformly believed that the process improvements initiated by this team could be replicated in other parts of the business and yield similar returns.

Isolating the Effects of the Intervention

How can you be sure that the gains or differences uncovered by your evaluation are attributable to the HPI intervention? Many factors can influence a particular business performance measure, so a rigorous and sound evaluation plan, especially at the ROI level, must include a method to isolate the effects of the program from other influences. Phillips (1997) cites several proven methods for doing just that:

- *Control groups:* With this design, the experimental group receives the intervention, the control group does not. Participants in both groups should be similar demographically and subjected to the same environmental influences. In this approach, measures taken after the intervention show the difference between the two groups that can be directly attributed to the intervention.

- *Trend line analysis:* With this approach, you draw a line from current performance to future performance, assuming that the current trend will continue even after the intervention. After the intervention, the postintervention performance is compared to the performance predicted on the trend line. A trend line analysis assumes that no new influences affected the situation. Advantages to this technique include its simplicity and cost effectiveness, although its primary disadvantage is in its potential inaccuracy.

- *Forecasting:* This approach is more analytical and mathematical than a trend line. When a mathematical relationship between input and output variables is known, an equation can be used to isolate effects. For example, if a single variable is influencing business results, the actual performance of the variable can be compared with the forecasted value after the intervention. Statistical models are required if several variables are involved.

- *Customer input:* This approach is used occasionally to determine the extent in which a planned intervention influenced the customer's decision to use a product or service. This technique is most useful for customer service and sales training.

- *Participants' and supervisors' estimates of intervention's effects:* Participants and supervisors estimate the extent to which identified improvements are directly related to the HPI intervention.
- *Expert estimation:* Experts estimate the extent to which identified improvements are directly related to the HPI intervention.

Remember, when estimates are sought, use the source that is most knowledgeable about the process and issues surrounding the value data. When using participant estimates as an approach to isolate the effects of your intervention, ensure that participants are capable of estimating the cost or value of the business units of measures being monitored and that they receive clear instructions and examples. Because participants are often the individuals closest to the improvement, they can be reliable data sources.

Converting Data to Monetary Value

After the isolation techniques are determined, level 4 data is converted to monetary value and compared with program costs. Data conversion requires placing a value on each unit of data associated with the intervention.

Ask these questions when you are converting data to monetary value:

- What is the value of one additional unit of production or service?
- What is the value of a reduction of one unit of quality measurement (cycle time, waste, error, process failure, call escalation)?
- What are the direct cost savings?
- What is the value of one unit of time improvement?
- Are cost records available?
- Is there a credible, internal expert who can estimate the value?
- Are supervisors capable of estimating the value?
- Is senior management willing to estimate the value?

Converting data to monetary value is integral to the ROI process and absolutely essential in calculating and communicating ROI results. To increase credibility, share responsibilities for this step, and use internal and external experts, historical costs, internal databases, supervisors, and managers to define standard improvement values. Finally, try to ensure that measurement and evaluation focus on the value of a single program or a few closely integrated interventions. When attempting to measure the effect of several courses in a series, it may be best to wait and evaluate the entire series as a whole. When evaluating a series conducted over a long period of time, the cause-and-effect relationship becomes more difficult to assess.

Reporting Results

Communicating results is as important as achieving them. Whether the report is a full impact study or a summary "white paper," it should include a background statement, a description of the evaluation strategy and data collected, an analysis of the findings, as well as assumptions used in the analysis.

Understand the needs of your audience and consider communication an ongoing process through which stakeholders are routinely informed and apprised of progress. Remember that credibility is always an issue when communicating program results. Credibility is influenced by the reputation of the source of the data and the reputation of the individual, group, or organization presenting the data.

Overcoming Barriers to Evaluation

Achieving a results-oriented evaluation strategy can be time consuming, labor intensive, and sometimes perceived as intrusive. Many barriers and false assumptions persist about implementing evaluation at the ROI level. Some of the more prevalent assumptions and their countermeasures are noted in table 11-3.

Your HPI Challenge

Through a conceptual overview, an established evaluation framework, a case study application, and related job aids, this chapter provided basic approaches for demonstrating to clients

Table 11-3. Some barriers posed by inaccurate assumptions about evaluation.

Assumption	Fact
A needs assessment takes too much time.	An intervention that is not based on a legitimate need will probably yield a poor result. Use just-in-time strategies and rely upon available data to analyze gaps and their causes.
ROI results will lead to criticism.	When approached as a continuous learning tool, practitioners are more likely to embrace a process that will help them assess program priorities and areas of impact.
ROI methods are too complex.	When implemented as a step-by-step process, evaluation at the ROI level is manageable and achievable for those motivated to persevere.
ROI is too expensive.	Phillips estimates that a comprehensive ROI process does not exceed more than 5% to 10% of an overall training or HRD budget when it is integrated properly with existing systems, used with an appropriate sampling of programs, and when responsibilities are shared in the implementation process.
Organization executives will require ROI for every project.	Not every program is appropriate for an ROI level of measurement. Set targets for evaluation at all levels. Work with stakeholders to establish selection criteria for determining which initiatives to evaluate at levels 4 and 5.
ROI is rarely used.	Benchmark with the more than 1,000 organizations around the world that use the ROI process and the 100-plus case studies published about its implementation.
It's not possible to isolate the influence of other factors.	There are at least 10 ways to isolate other factors when using the ROI process described here. The challenge is in selecting the right method(s) for any given situation.

the tangible and intangible returns of an HPI intervention. Upon completing this chapter, you will be able to

✓ define individual and organizational benefits to implementing a results-based evaluation strategy

✓ identify a proven model for conducting evaluation at the ROI level

✓ describe the steps required to build a credible, systemic evaluation plan

✓ apply a data collection template to an existing HPI project

✓ identify additional resources for enhancing evaluation skill sets.

Build credibility by continually developing your own evaluation skill sets. Leverage information, best practices, and tools and templates from the growing network of evaluation experts in the HPI field. The reality is that the message of a technically sound evaluation report is never good enough unless people believe the messenger. Recognize that your ability to increase organizational effectiveness with evaluation practices is directly correlated to your own level of confidence and competence with effective evaluation strategies.

References

Kirkpatrick, D.L. (1998). *Evaluating Training Programs: The Four Levels* (2d edition). San Francisco: Berrett-Koehler.

Phillips, J.J. (1997). *Return on Investment in Training and Performance Improvement Programs.* Houston: Gulf Publishing.

Rothwell, W.J. (1996). *ASTD Models for Human Performance Improvement.* Alexandria, VA: ASTD.

Additional Resources

Burkett, H. (2001). "Program Process Improvement Teams." *In Action: Return on Investment, 3.* Alexandria, VA: ASTD.

Burkett, H., and P. Phillips. (2001). "Managing Evaluation Shortcuts." *Info-line,* Issue No. 0111. Alexandria, VA: ASTD.

Hodges, T.K. (2002). *Linking Learning and Performance.* Boston: Butterworth Heinemann.

Parry, S.B. (1997). *Evaluating the Impact of Training.* Alexandria, VA: ASTD.

Phillips, J.J. (1997). *Handbook of Training Evaluation and Measurement Methods* (3d edition). Houston: Gulf Publishing.

Phillips, J.J. (February, 1996). "Was It the Training?" *T&D, 50*(2), 42–47.

Phillips, J.J., and P.F. Pulliam. (1999). "Level 5 Evaluation: Mastering ROI." *Info-line* Issue No. 9805. Alexandria, VA: ASTD.

ROI Network Website. www.roinetwork.org.

Rossett, A. (1999). *First Things Fast: A Handbook for Performance Analysis.* San Francisco: Jossey-Bass/Pfeiffer.

Rothwell, W.J. (1996) *Models for Human Performance Improvement: Roles, Competencies, and Outputs.* Alexandria, VA: ASTD.

About the Author

Holly Burkett, principal, Evaluation Works, has more than 18 years of progressive achievement in managing, designing, and evaluating diverse HRD and performance improvement initiatives. A senior professional in human resources (SPHR) and a certified ROI professional, she assists such organizations as Apple Computer, CALTRANS, the County of Sacramento, the University of California at Davis, and Premera Blue Cross in aligning performance initiatives with desired business results.

Burkett is an elected board member of the ROI Network and a frequent conference presenter on evaluation best practices. Her publications include case studies with ASTD's *In Action* series (2002, 2001, 1999); "Managing Evaluation Shortcuts," written with Patti Phillips for ASTD's *Info-line* (2001); and featured profiles as a best practice provider of ROI methodologies in both *T&D* and the Japanese *HRM and Training Magazine* (2000).

She earned her master of arts degree in human resources and organization development from the University of San Francisco. Burkett may be reached by telephone or fax at 530.756.1906 or by email at burketth@earthlink.net.

Performance Consultant— The Job

Dana Gaines Robinson

Key Points

> The job of a performance consultant is unique, entailing responsibilities and accomplishments that are different from those associated with other jobs.

> The work of a performance consultant is based largely on four key results, or accomplishments.

> Performance consultants identify leaders within the organization with whom they develop consultative business partnerships.

> On average, performance consultants spend about 25 percent of their time performing various analyses.

> Performance consultants must develop strong networks—within and without the organization—because it is not possible for one person to be an expert in all solutions that may be required in a performance change initiative.

What is a performance consultant, otherwise known as an account manager, relationship manager, business partner, or performance technologist? How do the day-to-day activities of a performance consultant differ from those carried out by someone who is, for example, an OD consultant, an HR specialist, or a learning consultant?

To understand more fully the job of performance consultant as it is being performed in organizations within North America, Partners in Change has conducted extensive interviews for the past five years on an annual basis with people who either are performance consultants or who manage these individuals. With five years of history, it is now possible to identify trends within the job and to identify the key results, or accomplishments, that are the focus of the job. It is important to note the parameters within which this information has been obtained:

- Information has been obtained from people who work within an organization and not from external consultants.
- Information is from public and for-profit organizations within the United States and Canada; no data is obtained from organizations outside of North America.

Performance Consultant Defined

The career of performance consultant is on a growth curve—no doubt about that. More and more people list this job title on their business cards. Nevertheless, not everyone bearing the title of performance consultant is one! Performance consulting is more than delivering a different kind of training, as some would believe. Performance consulting entails responsibilities and accomplishments that are unique. Consider this definition:

A performance consultant partners with clients in an organization for the purpose of enhancing workplace performance in support of business goals.

What does this definition really mean? Take a closer look at some of the words and phrases. The verb *partners* indicates that the individual is collaborative and consultative to people in the organization and uses influence to guide decision making. The *client* is the person or people who own the business need supported by the work being done. *Enhancing workplace performance* means that the performance consultant holds no bias for or against any particular solutions and, instead, focuses on outputs or results. Generally these results are within the work system, inclusive of both the people and the work environment that must support these individuals. *Business goals* refer to the operational—even strategic—objectives for an entity such as a business unit, group, function, or the entire enterprise. Everything a performance consultant works on is designed to support directly the accomplishment of these goals.

So, What Does a Performance Consultant Do?

Overall, there are four key results that comprise the majority of work for a performance consultant. Table 12-1 lists these results; more information about each follows.

Key Result: Form and Build Partnerships With Clients

Performance consultants build relationships with key clients (owners of business needs) independent of project work. Therefore, performance consultants identify leaders within the organization with whom a businesslike, consultative partnership should be developed.

Who are these leaders? Performance consultants indicate that they build partnerships with individuals who are presidents, vice presidents, senior vice presidents, directors, and managers of large functions or departments. When specific leaders have been identified, performance consultants take the initiative to nurture the relationship, even though there may be no project work to be done at that time.

Table 12-1. Key results accomplished by performance consultants.

Key Result	Description
Form and build partnerships with clients	Identify and develop relationships with key individuals in the organization independent of project work.
Complete performance analyses	Identify and report performance requirements, performance gaps, and causes of gaps through the use of reliable data collection methods and sources.
Manage performance change projects	Plan, organize, and monitor work done by others in support of projects to enhance performance of people within the organization.
Measure impact of the solutions	Evaluate the change in business results, job performance, and/or work environment factors resulting from the solutions that have been implemented.

These partnerships are established over a period of time and require that the performance consultant become very knowledgeable in the business of the client. Performance consultants report that they read business documents and stay current with journals and other publications that specialize in business news. They also attend staff meetings of their clients to hear first-hand about relevant business issues, and they "shadow" people in various jobs within the client's organization to learn more about what is required to successfully perform in those jobs.

To provide some indication of how substantial this key result is, performance consultants indicate they spend, on average, 16 percent of their job time—or more than 35 days in a year—performing this result. They also indicate that the number of leaders with whom they develop sustained partnerships, is eight. In other words, performance consultants are investing time in partnerships with these eight individuals, even when there is no project work to be done. It is through these partnerships, based upon mutual trust and access, that performance consultants gain proactive entry into work opportunities.

Key Result: Complete Performance Analyses

It is not possible to enhance workplace performance without obtaining data; front-end work is mandatory, not optional. Performance consultants spend, on average, about 25 percent of their time in this result area. In some instances, the performance consultant designs, collects, and reports results from performance assessments. In other cases, performance consultants broker this work to others, assuming more of a project manager role.

What's interesting is the variety of performance assessments that are undertaken. In total, there are six unique assessments completed by a majority of the performance consultants who were interviewed. These are listed in table 12-2, together with the percentage of performance consultants who indicate they are providing this type of assessment service.

Clearly, the word *assessment* is too general to describe what is done by performance consultants because they are using so many different types of assessments. One of the skills required by performance consultants is the ability to identify the appropriate assessment for the situation at hand.

Key Result: Manage Performance Change Projects

As noted earlier, a performance consultant should not have any bias for or against any solution or intervention. For the most part, performance consultants do not design and implement solutions such as training, compensation,

Table 12-2. Types of performance assessments provided by performance consultants.

Type of Assessment	Percentage of Performance Consultants Providing This Assessment
Process/Workflow Models Designing the work process required to produce needed outputs	65%
Performance Models Defining required results and best practices	70%
Competency Models Defining required skill, knowledge, and attributes	70%
Gap Analyses Defining current performance compared to required performance	95%
Cause Analyses Determining reasons for performance gaps	80%
Learning Needs Assessment Identifying skill and knowledge deficits to be addressed	87%

or team building. Rather, they broker people into the project who have this expertise. Performance consultants then manage the project. The analogy that is frequently used is that of orchestra leader; a performance consultant, working with a client, orchestrates people into and out of the initiative. Types of projects managed by performance consultants include

- formation of learning solutions
- design and implementation of a performance management system
- development of job aids and templates
- modification of compensation and other incentive systems
- clarification of roles between people in different jobs.

It is not possible for one person to be an expert in all the solutions that may be required in a performance change initiative. Therefore, performance consultants have developed strong networks—within and outside the organization—upon which they can draw as the situation warrants. On average, performance consultants manage eight performance change projects a year; some of these are large in scope, and some are small. The time required in a year to focus on this key result is 35 percent.

Key Result: Measure the Impact of Solutions

In the ongoing research being conducted at Partners in Change, this key result has only recently become the focus of inquiry. Therefore, the information about this result is not as substantial as for the other three. Nevertheless, it does appear that most performance consultants are focusing on this result. Seventy percent indicate they are measuring performance change following the implementation of solutions designed to change performance; 45 percent indicate they are measuring operational results. The median amount of time spent in this result area is five percent, so it is clearly the area of least focus in the job.

A Snapshot of the Performance Consultant's Job

Figure 12-1 summarizes what is known about key results focused upon by performance consultants. Table 12-3 provides some additional information including the trend, which has been identified during the five years of research.

Selection Criteria

When selecting people into the job of performance consultant, there is some variability regarding the type of experience that is preferred. Many individuals indicate they seek people who have three to five years' experience in HR, HPI, or training and development. Others indicate they value people who have worked in the line organization. These individuals bring the business experience to the job; in some cases, these people also bring client relationships to the job.

The possession of a bachelor's degree is generally valued, but a master's degree or doctorate is usually not required. Finally, there are competencies that are vital to success in this job. Table 12-4 lists competencies that are used to select people into the job. This table is a composite list of all competencies identified by at least half of the performance consultants who were interviewed.

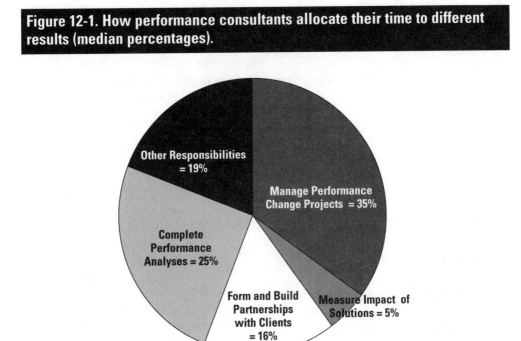

Figure 12-1. How performance consultants allocate their time to different results (median percentages).

Table 12-3. Summary of key results for a performance consultant.

Key Result	Comments
Form and build partnerships with clients	• Partnerships are developed independent of project work and with people who are in the middle and upper levels in organizations. • Average number of partnerships: 8 • Trend: Constant
Complete performance analyses	• There are six unique types of assessments that are completed; most performance consultants are prepared to provide any of these six assessments as the situation warrants. • Trend: Slight increase in time being spent.
Manage performance change projects	• Performance consultants rarely design and deliver solutions; rather, they broker people into the project who have this expertise. • Average number of projects managed in a year: 8 • Trend: Constant

(continued next page)

Table 12-3. Summary of key results for a performance consultant. *(continued)*

Key Result	Comments
Measure the impact of the solutions	• Approximately half of performance consultants are measuring performance change and operational impact following solution implementation. • Trend: Too early to tell

Table 12-4. Competencies needed by performance consultants.

Technical/Process Competence

1. Analysis Skill: Obtaining, synthesizing, and reporting data (both narrative and quantitative).

2. Business Knowledge: Knowledge of how businesses function and achieve success; knowledge of these factors for the organization(s) specifically being supported.

3. Change Management Skill: Guiding others to identify and take required actions in support of a performance change initiative.

4. Facilitation Skill: Managing meetings and group processes to ensure that the objectives of the group are achieved.

5. HPI Understanding: Knowledge of HPI as a discipline, as well as knowledge of the work of those who are its primary leaders and thinkers.

6. Influencing Skill: Encouraging acceptance to an idea through interpersonal skills and persuasion.

7. Project Management Skill: Planning, organizing, and monitoring work done by others in support of a specific project or assignment.

8. Questioning Skill: Gathering information through the process of interviews and other probing methods.

9. Relationship-Building Skill: Establishing and maintaining collaborative partnerships with individuals across a broad range of people and groups.

10. Systematic Thinking Skill: Viewing the organization as a system, recognizing that the success of the whole is dependent upon the integration, understanding and inclusion of all segments.

Attributes

1. Behavioral Flexibility: Readiness to modify approach or performance when required.

2. Comfort With Ambiguity: Demonstrating comfort in situations where the goals or process to achieve goals are unclear and difficult to determine.

3. Objectivity: Maintaining a bias-free approach to situations and people.

4. Self-Confidence: Managing own performance in an effective manner when placed in new or challenging situations.

As you can see, the listed competencies fall into two categories:

- *Technical/process competence:* Competencies that can be developed.
- *Attributes:* Competencies that are actually characteristics or traits and are, therefore, difficult to develop; they should be identified at the time of selection.

Compensation Issues

Responses to queries about compensation yielded a wide range of responses. The lowest annual compensation figure provided was $30,000; the highest was $175,000, including a bonus. By averaging the low figures and the high figures for year 2000 salaries, the following mean range was identified: $44,700 to $76,300. It should be noted that this compensation assumes the performance consultant is an individual contributor and not a manager of others.

Example

Perhaps it would be helpful to look at an example of a performance consultant performing some of the results and responsibilities described in this chapter.

The organization is a large insurance company. It recently acquired another, smaller company. The two companies had different cultures and systems. There were morale and performance problems that were becoming more severe by the day. The most pressing problems were the backlog of work, claims not being processed in a timely manner, and dissatisfied customers.

The performance consultant and client (the regional claims manager) agreed it would be good to understand the problem more fully before determining what actions to take. The performance consultant designed and completed a cause analysis to determine the root causes for the performance and morale problems. Information was obtained by interviewing and observing adjustors and the supervisor of these individuals. Letting the data speak for itself, the performance consultant met with the client to review the information. It was agreed the root causes for the problem were the following:

- The number of claims that required processing since the acquisition had tripled; however, the staff had been reduced in numbers because of a layoff before the acquisition.

- The work process was flawed in that there was a bottleneck. Currently all processed work had to flow through one individual who was overloaded.
- There were many people from the acquired insurance organization who had not been provided with the skills and knowledge needed to work within the system—a system that was new to them.
- The supervisor's work style was autocratic, causing many of the morale problems in evidence.

Working together, the performance consultant and client decided to reengineer the claims process to remove the bottleneck. Additionally, people from the acquired organization were developed and the supervisor coached so his work style became more collaborative. Another option, to hire more people, was not feasible.

All recommendations were implemented, with the performance consultant working to manage the change initiative. The backlog of work has been removed, customer satisfaction has improved, and the two groups have integrated into one team.

Your HPI Challenge

Would you like to be a performance consultant? How skillful and prepared are you to be successful in this role? The readiness assessment in figure 12-2 is based upon the results of a performance consultant as described in this chapter. Using the key at the bottom of the page, rate your skill level for each listed performance requirement.

Figure 12-2. Rate your readiness to enter the field of performance consulting.

	My Current Level of Competence		
Form and Build Partnerships With Clients This output includes the following:	**Proficient**	**Adequate**	**Basic**
✓ Initiate meetings with clients (i.e., owners of business needs) to discuss *performance* implications of *business needs.*			
✓ Reframe requests for training/other solutions into requests for HPI.			
✓ "Push back" when what the client is requesting will not achieve the results as stated.			
Complete Performance Analyses This output includes the following:			
✓ Contract for completion of performance assessments with clients.			
✓ Form:			
Process models			
Performance models			
Competency models			
✓ Determine gaps between desired and current performance (conduct gap analysis).			
✓ Identify work environment factors affecting performance (conduct cause analysis).			
✓ Influence clients to take all actions required to enhance performance.			
Manage Performance Change Projects This output includes the following:			
✓ Organize resources to accomplish performance change initiatives.			
✓ Work with clients to select appropriate interventions to address root causes of problem.			
✓ Coordinate task teams formed to redesign work environment systems and processes.			
✓ Oversee the progress of task teams working on projects.			

(continued next page)

Figure 12-2. Rate your readiness to enter the field of performance consulting. *(continued)*

	My Current Level of Competence		
Measure Impact of the Solutions This output includes the following:	**Proficient**	**Adequate**	**Basic**
✓ Develop a measurement plan, obtaining client support for this plan.	_____	_____	_____
✓ Gather and analyze measurement data.	_____	_____	_____
✓ Report measurement results to clients.	_____	_____	_____

Rating Key:

Proficient = I consistently demonstrate skill in handling typical, unique, and difficult situations.

Adequate = I demonstrate skill in typical work situations but will require coaching on how to apply the skill in new or challenging situations.

Basic = I have only foundation skills in this area.

Additional Resources

Bellman, G.M. (1990). *The Consultant's Calling: Bringing Who You Are to What You Do.* San Francisco: Jossey-Bass.

Block, P. (2000). *Flawless Consulting: A Guide to Getting Your Expertise Used* (revised edition). San Diego: Pfeiffer & Company.

Broad, M., and J. Newstrom. (1992). *Transfer of Training.* Reading, PA: Addison-Wesley.

Chang, R.Y., and P. De Young. (1996). *Measuring Organizational Improvement Impact: A Practical Guide to Successfully Linking Organizational Improvement Measures.* Irvine, CA: Richard Chang Associates.

Dean, P.J., and D.E. Ripley. (1997). *Performance Improvement Pathfinders: Models for Organizational Learning Systems.* Washington, DC: International Society for Performance Improvement.

Fuller, J. (1997). *Managing Performance Improvement Projects: Preparing, Planning, and Implementing.* San Francisco: Pfeiffer & Company.

Gilbert, T.F. (1978). *Human Competence: Engineering Worthy Performance.* New York: McGraw-Hill.

Hale, J.A. (1998). *The Performance Consultant's Fieldbook: Tools and Techniques for Improving Organizations and People.* San Francisco: Pfeiffer & Company.

Kirkpatrick, D.L. (1998). *Evaluating Training Programs: The Four Levels* (2d edition). San Francisco: Berrett-Koehler.

Robinson, D.G., and J.C. Robinson (editors). (1998). *Moving From Training to Performance: A Practical Guidebook.* Alexandria, VA: ASTD and Berrett-Koehler.

Robinson, D.G., and J.C. Robinson. (1995). *Performance Consulting: Moving Beyond Training.* San Francisco: Berrett-Koehler.

Rossett, A. (1999). *First Things Fast: A Handbook for Performance Analysis.* San Francisco: Jossey-Bass/Pfeiffer.

Rummler, G.A., and A.P. Brache. (1995). *Improving Performance: How to Manage the White Space on the Organization Chart.* San Francisco: Jossey-Bass.

Scott, B. (2000). *Consulting on the Inside: An Internal Consultant's Guide to Living and Working Inside Organizations.* Alexandria, VA: ASTD.

Stolovitch, H.D., and E.J. Keeps (editors). (1992). *Handbook of Human Performance Technology: A Comprehensive Guide for Analyzing and Solving Performance Problems in Organizations.* San Francisco: Jossey-Bass.

Sugrue, B., and J. Fuller. (1999). *Performance Interventions: Selecting, Implementing, and Evaluating the Results.* Alexandria, VA: ASTD.

Zemke, R., and T. Kramlinger. (1982). *Figuring Things Out.* Reading, PA: Addison-Wesley.

About the Author

Dana Gaines Robinson, president of Partners in Change, is a recognized leader in the area of performance technology. With coauthor Jim Robinson, she wrote the books *Training for Impact: How to Link Training to Business Needs and Measure the Results* (Jossey-Bass, 1989) and *Performance Consulting: Moving Beyond Training* (Berrett-Koehler, 1995). The Robinsons also edited a third book, *Moving From Training to Performance: A Practical Guidebook* (ASTD and Berrett-Koehler, 1998). Their most recent book is *Zap the Gaps! Target Higher Performance and Achieve It!* (HarperCollins, 2002), cowritten with Ken Blanchard.

Robinson has a bachelor's degree in sociology from the University of California and a master's degree in psychoeducational processes from Temple University. In 1999, she was awarded the Distinguished Contribution Award for Workplace Learning and Performance by ASTD. You may contact her via email at drobinson@partners-in-change.com.

Afterword

So now you know what HPI is and how it is applied from analysis through evaluation. Does that mean it's time for you to order new business cards that say "Performance Consultant" below your name? Well...maybe. By reading this book you have certainly become familiar with the essentials of HPI. You've learned

- the HPI model
- how a business analysis begins the process and provides a basis for a credible HPI approach
- the way performance analysis links business goals to organizational performance
- methods for performing gap and cause analyses
- the use of a client/consultant team to create effective interventions
- the three major categories of interventions and where they are used
- how to implement HPI interventions by involving stakeholders
- methods for evaluating HPI interventions
- what an HPI practitioner actually does on the job.

But where do you go from here? If HPI has captured your attention, you might want to try one or more of these steps:

- Use the resources listed at the end of each chapter to learn more about HPI topics that are of the most interest or relevance to you.
- Pick an area of HPI that you want to become an expert in and study it in detail through books, magazine articles, and interviews with practitioners.

- Broaden your HPI knowledge by learning more about the theory and history of HPI through the writings of the founding fathers and mothers of HPI: Joe Harless, Roger Kaufman, Dana Gaines Robinson, and Thomas Gilbert.

- If you feel that you are definitely ready to become an HPI practitioner, take the certification programs offered by either ASTD or ISPI.

- Register for an HPI seminar from one of the consulting organizations that provides them. The best of these will allow you to learn and practice a single area of HPI at a time, starting with analysis and working through to evaluation techniques.

- Find an HPI practitioner who will take you on as an apprentice. Nothing is better, or teaches you more, than the actual experience of performing in an HPI consultation, even if you spend most of the time simply observing.

- Ask your local HPI guru to tell you about the different HPI initiatives he or she has completed, how they were alike, how they differed, what worked, and what didn't.

With some proper planning and a bit of hard work, you can break out of the training mode and break into HPI. The decision is yours. No matter which path you choose, no doubt you will encounter interesting projects and make meaningful contributions to the organizations you serve.